P9-DCO-755

For Sandra

❀ ❀ ❀

In Memory of Clyde

# WHAT IF
# GOD
## WERE THE
# SUN?

## A NOVEL

## John Edward

Jodere Group, Inc.
San Diego, California

Copyright © 2000 by John Edward

**Published by:** Jodere Group, Inc., P.O. Box 910147,
San Diego, CA 92191-0147 • (800) 569-1002

**Distributed in the United States by:** Hay House, Inc.,
P.O. Box 5100, Carlsbad, CA 92018-5100 • (800) 654-5126
(800) 650-5115 (fax) • www.hayhouse.com

*Editorial:* Jill Kramer, Shannon Todd • *Design:* Summer McStravick

The original song "You Are Always Here with Me" has been used by permission of the composer. Copyright © 2000 by Wendy Esposito.

All rights reserved. No part of this book may be reproduced by any mechanical, photographic, or electronic process, or in the form of a phonographic recording; nor may it be stored in a retrieval system, transmitted, or otherwise be copied for public or private use— other than for "fair use" as brief quotations embodied in articles and reviews without prior written permission of the publisher. In the event you use any of the information in this book for yourself, which is your constitutional right, the author and the publisher assume no responsibility for your actions.

**Library of Congress Cataloging-in-Publication Data**

Edward, John (John J.)
    What if God were the sun : a novel / John Edward.
       p.  cm.
   ISBN 1-58872-003-9
     1. Death--Fiction.  I. Title.

PS3555.D82 W48 2000
813'.54--dc21

                          00-048656

ISBN 1-58872-003-9
03  02  01 00    6  5  4  3
1st printing, November 2000
3rd printing, December 2000

Printed in the United States of America

# Contents

*Prologue:* A Visit to a Loved One . . . . . . . . . ix

## PART I

**Chapter 1:** The Gift of Life. . . . . . . . . . . .3
**Chapter 2:** A Shadow Hangs Over Me. . . . .13
**Chapter 3:** The News. . . . . . . . . . . . . . .19
**Chapter 4:** Pictures in a Frame. . . . . . . . . 31
**Chapter 5:** Treasuring the Day . . . . . . . . . 37
**Chapter 6:** Songbirds, a Puppy,
and Home Movies . . . . . . . . . .43

## PART II

**Chapter 7:** Somewhere in Time. . . . . . . . . 59
**Chapter 8:** Best Friends Forever . . . . . . . . 77
**Chapter 9:** What If God Were the Sun? . . . . . 83

## PART III

**Chapter 10:** Going Home. . . . . . . . . . . . . . 111

*Epilogue:* A Happy Birthday, After All . . . . . .131

**About the Author** . . . . . . . . . . . . . . 145

# Prologue

## A Visit to a Loved One

I'm sitting here in the third-floor corridor of our local Community Hospital, counting the number of tiles that make up the bigger pattern on the floor. As I look around, I note that this complex feels more like a hotel than a medical center. The staff and administration are obviously interested in providing the best professional care they can, and it's clear that they also appreciate aesthetics. The manicured bushes, plants, trees, and flower gardens are exquisite, and they're accented by stately fountains bubbling with softly flowing water. The entire place is immaculate—and gives off a feeling of efficiency and security—to inpatients, outpatients, and even visitors like me.

I walk into 314, a double room, and see that the patient in the other bed is having a chest x-ray, so I decide to wait outside.

"It should only be a minute, and then you can come right back in and visit," the red-haired radiology technician says, smiling at me.

She pushes the portable x-ray machine into the room toward her patient, and yells out, "Mr. Brown? Are you awake?"

I feel like yelling out, "Are you kidding?!" The sound of the machine being noisily wheeled into the room will more than take care of that. And, of course, when Mr. Brown sees the technician coming toward him, he'll really perk up. She's quite attractive.

Back out in the hall again, I find it amazing that the mind can find the smallest way to occupy itself. I can't believe I'm taking the time to notice the tiny gold specks swirled into the smaller interlocked triangles that form the squares in the floor tile. But what else am I supposed to do in a hospital? It's either count the floor tiles or do battle with the vending machines.

Maybe I should make another attempt to fight with the soda-and-snack dispenser down the hall. At last count, the machines were winning. Let's see, I believe that for my five-dollar investment, the return was two cans of Pepsi and a bag of Famous Amos chocolate chip cookies. What a bargain. Not only am I out a few bucks, but there goes my low-carb diet. Maybe all those little money-munching, profit-making machines around the hospital go toward buying those beautiful fountains. Who knows?

Then again, maybe I need to focus on getting more than three hours of sleep at night. I'm very tired, and I'm being a little sarcastic and cynical. I know one thing, though: No matter how phenomenal a place this might be, I don't want to be here. I'm not happy about this visit—not happy at all.

It's funny how rules can mean so much to one person and so little to another. The first day I came here, I walked past the front desk and went right up to room 314. Almost immediately, I was verbally assaulted by one of the many blue-haired Rambo wannabes. You know the ones I mean—the women with the stern eyes and pointy index fingers that they wag in your face.

This particular "enforcer" stopped me in my tracks, informing me that I was in "breach of hospital security."

"Do you think you're special?" she barked. "There are rules, you know."

All of this because I didn't get a room pass. After I expressed my deepest apologies for putting the lives

of 200 patients at risk by not securing the large plastic card with 314 on it, I assured her that I would never
violate the rules again. Nope—never again would I
walk past the front desk on my way upstairs. So . . .
I made sure that I found every side and back door
possible to get up there from that day forward. I have
been here every day since then. And that was two
weeks ago.

It's times like these that force you to be a little
more analytical about life. Not the kind of analysis
that requires a visit to the local therapist and a nice
black couch, but a more personal type of introspec-
tion where you delve into the meaning of your own exis-
tence. I believe that it's times like these when your faith
is stretched and tested.

When you think about life, you can't help realizing how much humor and irony there is all around you.
It's right there, right in front of your face. And sometimes it takes a personal epiphany to get that sort of
reality check. Well, mine is happening as I sit here,
but it's not so subtle. It's screaming out reminders about
personal decisions I made in the past.

All of a sudden, the act of visiting one of my parents in the hospital has rules and regulations attached
to it—not to mention a time limit. Somehow this all
makes me think about the many holiday and Sunday

dinners that I neglected to be a part of because I was "busy" or just too tired or lazy to go to. I made up every excuse in the book not to attend those family functions, and sometimes I went to a holiday party at a friend's house instead.

Now it seems very ironic that those missed opportunities are truly being missed—more than ever.

As we go through life, we might make choices that we believe are important for us at that time. But when we least expect it, or when we're selfishly neglecting the situations in front of us, what I call a "pocket of emotion" is filled in with a feeling reminiscent of the experience that has passed. What we didn't realize at that time was that we would be dealing with that pocket of emotion at a later date, and usually at a time when we would be the most vulnerable.

That's how I feel right now. I didn't realize back then when I was avoiding those family functions that I was missing anything, and I took those opportunities to be with my loved ones for granted. And now I have regrets.

I'm feeling pretty morose as I go over all this in my mind, yet I clearly recognize that the past is the past. So here I am in the present, counting floor tiles and realizing that my heart's "pocket of feeling" is being emptied. Too bad it isn't more like placing my hand in an old jacket pocket and finding a $20 bill. Instead, there's just emotion.

One of the nicer women at the front desk is approaching me, and I'm afraid that she's going to throw me out or at least make an attempt. My parents taught me to be respectful of people who are older than I am, but nobody is going to tell me when and for how long I can see the person who loved and raised me. Instead, she just smiles at me, in a very compassionate and understanding manner. It seems like she knows something I don't. But maybe I'm just grasping at straws—I'm so exhausted I can't think straight.

Once you make it past the army of perfume-packing seniors at the front desk, then the nurses on the units are next. Some of them are so busy that they don't care if you sleep in the same room as the patients. Many of them even feel secure, knowing that you're right there with your loved ones. Then, if something happens, you can notify the nurse's station immediately.

Of course there are a few nurses who take great offense as to why you're constantly questioning the care your family member is receiving, or every pill and injection that's being administered. But for the most part, the nurses are all supportive of relatives being here. We all know that in many cases, like this one, it's just a matter of time.

For the past two weeks, I've been having a hard time trying to figure out what to do all day at a place like this. Do I buy flowers or stuffed animals at the gift shop that say "Get Well Soon"? Maybe take a chance and buy some raffle tickets at the Ladies' Auxiliary desk? Or, do I just deal with the harsh reality of what I instinctively know to be true, but can't seem to allow myself to deal with? You know the harsh reality I'm talking about: the one that tells you that the person you're visiting may not be there the next time you walk into their room.

On my left, on a stretcher sitting in the hall, there's a woman who looks to be at least 80 years old. She's lying there coiled up in a fetal position, screaming for someone, anyone, to help her. Her pleas seem to be going unanswered, though, and it's heartbreaking to listen to. I walk over to give her some comfort while I wait to go back into room 314, yet it's clear that she's suffering from some form of dementia or Alzheimer's disease.

I wonder if she has any family. Do they come to see her, or has she been abandoned here, doomed to spend her last days in and out of the local nursing home and hospital? I couldn't imagine ever abandoning my mother like that.

That's when I remember once again why I come here, day after day, hour after hour. I hate the fact that circumstances have forced me to be here on and off over the last two weeks. In the circle of life, you know that this day will arrive. You talk about it as if it's far in the future, and you plan for it with health insurance and life insurance and wills, yet you never really discuss death in detail with the people around you. If you were to do that, somebody would tell you to shut up, that you're being morbid.

"Code 999 K3! Code 999 K3!" I'm jolted out of my reverie by the screeching voice on the hospital's PA system.

It sounds as if a herd of elephants is coming toward me. The air seems to rumble with noise and energy, and I can feel the atmosphere literally changing around me. I look to my left and right, up and down the corridor, to see what all the fuss is about. It is at this moment that the large wooden doors with the big glass panels down the hall to my left burst open. The blur of white lab coats goes rushing by me into room 314. My heart starts to pound, and I can feel my adrenaline start to rush.

I'd seen a code 999 once before. I know that it's like a race for time, a race for life—like a gun going off and they're all competing to save someone.

As I'm breaking out into a cold sweat, the brutal reality of what's happening smacks me right in the face, and my eyes start welling up, yet I'm frozen to my spot. I can't seem to get my body to move closer to the door. Four, five, and now at least seven people are cramming into room 314. Nurses, respiratory therapists, and various technicians are all crowding in there—and I can see the crash cart being wheeled in.

Jamie, my favorite nurse, who usually makes me laugh by winking at me and constantly droning, "I gotta get outta this place. . . . ," is scurrying into the room, too, with a very concerned expression on her face.

The way that she glances at me as she runs in worries me more than anything. My heart is pounding even harder, and I'm starting to feel lightheaded.

No . . . it's not Mr. Brown who's having the medical emergency!

As hot tears flow uncontrollably from my eyes, I think, *Oh my God, this is what it feels like to lose a parent . . . and today of all days . . . when we should be celebrating a birthday!*

❀ ❀ ❀

# Part I

# Chapter One

## The Gift of Life

*Today is the milestone of my daughters'
seventh birthday. It is with gratitude that I
look around at the neighborhood and the
family that I have loved my entire life. Yet
despite all of my blessings, something troubling is churning within me. . . .*

I'm standing at the window, watching the latest group
of family members arrive for today's party. I
couldn't have asked for a more perfect summer day.
The sky is a beautiful blue, with not a cloud to be
seen for miles. This ideal weather has made planning
the party today a lot easier. I don't have to worry about
rain, or where we will entertain the 50 or 60 people

who are going to be milling in and out of our house today.

As I look up and down our block, I see the lovely elm trees lining the street, shedding some much-needed shade on the parked cars filling our block. Thank God that our neighbors understand that we have a large Italian-American family, and celebrating birthdays is just another excuse to invite as many people over as possible. Our neighbors are used to not being able to park in front of their own homes on days like these.

Even though today's festivities are to celebrate the joint birthday of my seven-year-old twin girls, the entire family has been invited. Not only will they all show up, but they'll bring their extended family, in-laws, and even friends. All guests in our home are considered family. "Bring them all over" is what Grandma Rosie always said. *Invite all your friends and their family* was her motto; it's the way that she brought us up. The fun part for the girls today is that the guests are bearing gifts. The fun part for the *grown-ups* is that they're also bearing wine, food, and desserts. We've already filled up two large tables with different salads, pastas, breads, and delectable sweets.

Aunt Gina, my mom's older sister, is the latest arrival, and she's walking up the driveway waving her hands to the group of adults sitting on the lawn furniture on the patio. Aunt Gina is carrying birthday gifts for the girls, and her daughter, Phyllis, is right behind her with *her* daughter, Katrina. My cousin Phyllis and I are only a few years apart in age, but she married earlier than I did. Katrina is her only child and is beginning her first year of high school in a week. Looking at her makes me feel like time is moving too fast. It seems like only yesterday that Phyllis and I were harassing Grandma Rosie about her famous Italian meatballs. I liked them *without* raisins, and Phyllis seemed to like them *with*. It was a constant battle to see which one of us could get Grandma to cook them the "right" way.

As I walk away from the window in the kitchen that overlooks the street and the front lawn, I remember that I forgot to go next door and invite our neighbor Eileen over. She is family to all of us. My wife, Melissa, and I have tried to be there for her over the last few years. Eileen has had a difficult time of it since the accidental death of her husband, Frankie. They moved in years ago, shortly after Grandma Rosie bought this old house with Grandpa Jack, and our two families have developed a strong bond. Even though we're not related by blood, we *are* related by the length of our friendship and the good times we've had. Eileen's daughter, Susan, or "Sooz," as I nicknamed her, regard each other as family. If fact, we're as close as a brother and sister.

Being that this house has been in the family for years, I can't even begin to guess how many parties it has seen. Boy, if walls could talk, the stories that these would tell! So much history—positive and negative—and all the laughter and tears, the triumphs and tragedies, all here at 11 North Field Road, in good old Glen Cove, Long Island.

In years past, Glen Cove was viewed as a wealthy area in which to live, nestled far up on the North Shore of Long Island, New York, at one time nicknamed the "Gold Coast." Today it's a city made up of a diverse mix of ethnic groups and cultures. When my family first moved here from Brooklyn some 40 years ago, I believe that besides the trees and dirt roads, it was largely an Italian community, or at least that was how my family viewed it.

Now, the trees are mostly gone, and in their place are the usual things you find in any American suburb: residential homes, apartment complexes, senior centers, a local police department, and a town square with its very own city hall. Glen Cove even has several multiplex movie theaters, and, of course, the requisite strip malls and fast-food joints. Unfortunately, it has also seen the closing of the Mom-and-Pop-type video stores and corner markets, and in their place, the Blockbuster video superstores and huge supermarkets now stand. I suppose that's called "progress." But it's all relative, isn't it?

What Glen Cove *is* known for are the fine upscale restaurants such as La Pace and La Ginestra. People from all over come here to tempt their taste buds with the finest of cuisines. Because of its large Italian population, my town has also become well known for Italian delis such as Razzanos and Iavarone Brothers, where you can wait in line for hours to be served. But it's worth it once you get a whiff of the delicious meats, cheeses, sauces, and other delicacies.

And I can't forget to mention the greatest meal served in all of Long Island—the feast of St. Rocco's Church. The last week in July, the streets all around the church are jam-packed with people who travel from all over the island to pay tribute to St. Rocco; and to play carnival games, gamble a bit, listen to the Italian-American singers in the Tivoli bakery garden adjacent to the church, and, naturally, to get a bag full of zeppolis, little fried pieces of dough that are covered with powdered sugar. I sure hope someone brings them to today's party. They can't be good for you, but boy, do they ever taste amazing. I'm told that even right before Grandma Rosie died, she had my mom and Aunt Gina go down to the feast to get her a bag of them.

Yup—Glen Cove is where I live, and I wouldn't live anywhere else in the world.

Before I go any further, let me take this opportunity to introduce myself. My name is Timothy Callahan, and this is my story. I'm going to tell you a little bit about how I learned about life, love, death, and God—you know, everything in life that really matters.

With all my references to being Italian, you're probably wondering how I ended up in an Italian family with a name like Callahan, instead of some melodious Italian name ending with a vowel. Well, my father is of Irish descent, and my mother is Italian. However, my heritage and traditional values have mostly been passed down to me from my mother's side of the family.

The Callahan branch has always been more reserved and unemotional. My mom tried to integrate this Irish side with that of the Martonas' (my mom's maiden name), but they just never meshed. Kind of like oil and vinegar. When I would hear my mom and my maternal Grandmother Rosie talk about my father's side of the family and how my mom tried to get them to participate in family activities, Grandma Rosie would always say, "You can't argue with a duck."

I guess what she meant to say was, "You tried your best, now leave it alone." She would refer to the Irish side of the family as unique and different, yet she seemed to understand their quirks. Whenever Grandma would make statements like that . . . well, I'm sure that to her, the phrase carried great meaning, but to the rest of us . . . we would just look at each other with stifled giggles. Maybe something got lost in the translation.

But then there were other sentiments that she expressed that were so profound that they've lasted in my family for generations. Oh, how I wish she were here to see my girls. They would adore her, and she would just eat them up.

I want to explain what's precipitating these ruminations on life and death. I'm going to be celebrating my 35th birthday in a few weeks, and I'm at a point where I'm looking at my life from the standpoint of the third person—wondering in awe how I got here and how it all happened. Wasn't it just yesterday that I was nine years old?

Anyway, I'm married to a beautiful and talented artist named Melissa, and together, we have twin girls: Rachel, named for my mother; and Victoria, named for a singer who was a friend of the family. As I said, the twins are celebrating their seventh birthday today.

For the last couple of years, Melissa and I have planned big bashes to celebrate our girls' birthday. We sort of feel that since the girls are twins, they don't each have their own unique and special day, so we need to compensate and make their dual birthday celebration twice as big. They don't seem to mind, and these parties have become more than just the usual birthday cake and pin-the-tail-on-the-donkey-type deals. They're really extravaganzas in their own right.

Melissa and I value our family members and their involvement in the girls' lives, so we use their birthday as a kind of reunion. Each year our home is filled with the sounds of children laughing and playing, adult men playing cards at the dining room table, and women collecting and gathering either in the kitchen or the backyard, gossiping about all the events that are happening in their lives.

I really need this party to be especially meaningful for all those who attend this year for two reasons. For one thing, the twins are getting the gift that they've begged us for over the last three years—the gift of life. No, not a new announcement of a baby on the way, but a little ball of unconditional love otherwise known as a puppy.

What's also different about this year is that I just found out that my mother has been diagnosed with a nontreatable form of cancer.

❋ ❋ ❋

# Chapter Two

## A Shadow Hangs Over Me

*I try to be strong, but I feel devastated. It seems that I can't help but think of all the others I've lost over the years. I'm overcome with mixed emotions and a sense of futility.*

Cancer. What a strange sound that word has. It seems that when words such as *tumor, malignant,* and *cancer* are spoken, the light of the day goes dim, and people start to speak in hushed tones. I don't think that they intend to act so strange, but they do. Maybe it's the fact that the word just forces people to reflect on the possibility that it could be *them* receiving that diagnosis. Or maybe it's because so many individuals die from cancer each year that there's a sense of hopelessness associated with the disease.

If you've ever known someone who has had to fight this dreaded battle for their own life, then you already know that the "cure" can also kill you. The frustration and mental agony associated with this knowledge is hard to take sometimes.

Originally, when the news first hit, I was hoping that Mom would be that miracle, the one person in a million who beats all the odds, the woman you see on TV talk shows with a bestselling book on how you can heal your life, while making a chocolate soufflé all the while. However, the doctors gently informed us that none of that would be taking place—no miracle, no book deal, and no soufflé.

As I look around the house I grew up in and now live in, I see a home with years of rich family history—it's also where my mom and *her* siblings grew up. I'm trying not to sink into despair, but as the noise of all the simultaneous conversations swirl around me, I am beset with an uncontrollable desire to scream. I feel a wild fury churning inside me, as I stifle the urge to yell, "Don't you people know that Mom is dying of cancer! How can you be so happy and act like everything is normal?!"

I refrain, of course, but it's weird having a thought so strong that I wonder if I might have actually said it. Especially when my Aunt Gina walks in and gives me a strange look. Now, not really being sure if I actually *did* utter my thoughts out loud, I quickly look around and realize that none of the activities around me have been disrupted. I glance once more at my mom's older sister in the doorway, and I greet her with as pleasant a smile as possible.

"Hey, Aunt G . . ." I eke out mildly, as I lean in to kiss her hello.

"Hey, yourself. Where's my sister?" Aunt Gina asks, with a concerned tone in her voice.

I now know that she's aware of what's going on. I bet my mother told her. I wonder who else here today knows or will be finding out today. I have so many mixed feelings and emotions. On the one hand, I want everyone to know what's happening so they can support my mom, but on the other hand, I don't want anything to put a downer on the upbeat party mood.

"Is she out back? Is she even here yet?" Aunt Gina questions, looking furtively to her left and right.

"Mom and Dad aren't here just yet. It's been a tough morning for them." I wait to see how Aunt Gina responds.

"I understand," she says simply. "We'll talk later. How are *you* doing? Where are Melissa and the girls?" She affirms my suspicions that she knows the truth about her sister, with her emphasis on the "you." Yet, she's also changing the subject so she doesn't have to get too involved in a conversation she wasn't happy delving into in the first place.

"Mel and the girls are hanging balloons in the backyard, and they're starting up the grill. Let me put that wine in the fridge so you can go and give the girls a big old hug," I say, as I grab the packages out of her hand. She silently walks out.

Coming from a family of just three kids, Gina, my mother, and my Uncle Claudio (who everyone called Clyde), were all very tight. My mother and sister became especially close after they lost Clyde a number of years ago. They've been inseparable ever since.

Gina's husband, Uncle Dominick, who died a couple of years ago from a massive heart attack, was a man of few words, but he possessed a big heart and enormous generosity and strength. If he were at the party today, he would be bringing in two or three cases of the best-tasting wine you could ever imagine. His entire life was devoted to building a very successful wine and liquor store, with distribution centers all over New York. He was the type of guy who would bring you a whole case of a certain wine if you expressed an interest in that variety. That was just his way.

Uncle Dominick had been the first person to die in our family for a number of years, and I remember that when he passed, my mom told me how lucky a family we were because there had been no deaths in our family for more than ten years.

It's a good thing she didn't know at the time how much heartache was to come.

❁ ❁ ❁

# Chapter Three

## The News

*As I stew in this terrible news, I remember the wisdom of my dear Grandma Rosie. I'm reminded of all of the life lessons she taught me, both in and out of church. The main message I keep coming back to is, "God is the Sun, Timmy . . ."*

The news. I keep referring to Mom's diagnosis as "the news." I only wish that this was like TV. You get into bed at the end of the day, and around 11 P.M., you turn on the nightly news. You see all the tragedies from the latest car crash to the blazing inferno that destroyed all the people in a certain apartment building. The negativity factor is huge, and you empathize with the families, but the truth is, you thank God that it's not you or yours. Then you hit the Power Off button on your television remote and you shut it out—it's over. You roll over and escape to the world of sleep.

But where is the "off" button in life? I don't have one I can hit right now. If I did, believe me, I would. Grandma Rosie always said, "Every knock is a boost, and God only gives us as much as we can handle—no more, no less. Most of all, we should be appreciative that He's sending these events our way. It's just His way of reminding us that He's up there watching."

I wonder if Grandma Rosie is up there watching today. Is she smiling sympathetically down at her daughter as she processes the harsh reality that the disease that took *her* life is now consuming her daughter? Where is God in all this? Is this fair?

Where are all the technological advances in medicine? You hear that they have this drug and that drug, but the doctor told us that there's nothing they can do for the type of cancer my mother has. A "pancoast tumor" is the diagnosis. A gross malignant mass to the apex of not one lung, but both. Normally, the doctor said, a person can live with this for months, even years, but because Mom's cancer has metastasized so quickly to the liver and pancreas, she may only have a few weeks left. We were informed that we should make arrangements and try to keep her as comfortable as possible.

How harsh those words were, ringing in my ears daily. The part that was the most difficult was hearing the doctor tell my mom that she had a fighting chance, and in a few weeks they would talk about treatment options, but that she needed to stay positive until then.

Melissa and I had taken Mom to the oncologist that day. I looked at Mel as she ran out of the doctor's waiting area to the ladies' room. It was too much for her to handle. My mother has been the only mom that Melissa has known over the last 15 years. Her mom died in childbirth, and her father crossed over when Mel was a sophomore in high school.

Even though the doctor basically lied directly to Mom's face, and tried to give her a few weeks of relaxed preparation to decide what her treatment options might be, I took one look at her, and her eyes told me that she knew. She would be a trooper and play this human charade for all concerned, but I could see that she was already planning to die.

Then I remember the time frame that the doctor had given me. It might only be "a few weeks"—

a few more weeks to be with my precious mother on this Earth. *A few weeks?! Make her comfortable? What if a few weeks isn't enough time?* I think to myself agonizingly.

I need . . . no, I *want*, more time. My girls are only seven years old. This means that their grandmother won't be a part of any future birthdays, sorrows and triumphs, graduations, and all the other firsts. Their Gramsy, as they refer to her, won't be at their Sweet Sixteen parties or be able to dance at their weddings.

I realize that I'm having purely selfish emotions as well. The hardest part is the realization that my 35th birthday is in a few weeks, and there's a possibility that Mom may die that very day. Wouldn't that be terrible? For someone in your family to die on your birthday? What would that mean?

Now that I'm festering in these morbid thoughts, I find myself thinking about my grandmother, too. I was around the same age as my girls when my Grandma Rosie died, but the impact that she had on my upbringing and beliefs is still intact today, some 30 years later. That thought brings me hope. Maybe the memories and words that their Gramsy has given my daughters will be forever etched in their minds, too.

Some words of wisdom from Grandmother Rosie come to me once again: "Timmy, I never thought I would be able to think back on the day you were born with any sort of happiness. Over 40 years ago, my mother, your great-grandmother, Louise, died on October 5th. That was one of the hardest losses for me to deal with. For years, whenever that date rolled around, I would find myself dreading it. I know that you probably don't want to hear that your birthday was special because of an unhappy event, but it was. Now, the only thing that gets me through it is knowing that that's the date when I saw your beautiful face for the first time."

I know that "fache bella" might actually be how she ended that sentiment, while pulling on both of my cheeks. Just the thought of that conversation makes my cheeks still hurt. Why is it that whenever some older Italian relative wants to prove a point or drive it home, they yell, slam their hand on the table for emphasis, or pinch your cheek as an endearment? I never really minded, though.

Death. It has such a final connotation. I remember first asking a priest about it during a mass in church, but not really getting an answer. Grandma Rosie used to drag me to church with her every day. Not just on Sundays for mass, but *every day!* That lasted until I started school, and then not too long after that, she died. That was my only happy memory connected with her death—not being dragged to church every single day. Hey, I was a typical kid.

I remember that Grandma Rosie would teach me all the rules about Jesus and God while we were at church. She had no choice. I was an inquisitive child who had questions about every situation I encountered.

"Why do we have to sit? Why do we have to stand? Why do we have to kneel?" I would whine.

But Grandma never lost her patience. She told me when I was *allowed* to sit and stand, and why I couldn't just walk into the pew and sit. She explained that I had to show my respect for being a guest in God's house, and the way that you did that was to make the sign of the cross and genu-flect at the entrance of the row.

What confused me the most was why I wasn't permitted to participate in the entire mass. I didn't comprehend why I wasn't allowed to have the cookie, or what everyone there called "the body" that the priest gave out. All those years of wait-ing to get my hands on one of those cookies . . .

I mean, it *had* to taste good, because people lined up single file in two columns at every mass to get just one. But just *one?* Who can eat just one cookie? No, that was unacceptable. As a child, I thought that I would need at least four or five.

Then I wanted to know what was in the gold cup. Every time I asked if it was milk, the lady at the reading pulpit on the altar would give me a stern look that told me to be quiet and stop asking all these questions.

If you're wondering why she was able to hear me, well, I was the kid who was always whispering so loudly that they could probably have heard me in the last pew. Not to mention that Grandma Rosie would never sit anywhere else but the first pew. (God forbid!) You'd think she was going to a concert or something, needing to be in God's front-row seat. It's not that she needed to see what was happening. There were never any surprises or additions to the service. Well, maybe a couple of new songs here and there, but for the most part, it was the same. I mean, I was able to memorize what the priest was going to do and say next without even paying attention. Which brings me to that day when I must have really embarrassed her.

I don't know what came over me, and my parents joked for years that Spirit must have moved me to do what I did, but on this one particular day, I suddenly stood up on the pew, closed my eyes and opened my arms outward, and started to yell the whole preamble that the priest used before the gospel—in perfect unison with him. I was great! I brought the house down. I stopped the mass completely, and even Father Sean laughed. He told my Grandma Rosie that I should think about being an altar boy. That was when the nasty lady who did one of the post-gospel readings walked over to me and forced me to sit in my place.

She gazed at me with her dark, evil eyes and pushed me down in the seat. Grandma referred to her afterwards and said, "The devil must have gotten into her to make her touch another person's child." That day, Grandma Rosie told this woman after mass that if she even so much as *looked* at me again in her presence, she'd be needing her last rites.

I remember feeling so vindicated when Grandma Rosie said that.

*You tell her, Grandma! Make her get on the ride last! That will teach her not to be mean,* I remember thinking to myself.

It took every ounce of self-control and discipline I had not to stick my tongue out at this mean woman who acted like she was the priest on the altar. I laugh now when I think about what Grandma Rosie actually said, and how she threatened this holy roller's life. I thought that it meant that when the church's big street festival began again, the mean lady would be forced to get on all the rides last . . . hence, "the last rides."

All of the small, seemingly insignificant incidents from my youth mean so much more to me today. But being just a little kid, they seemed to go right over my head at that time. I wondered about some of the other things that Grandma said back then, too.

After asking one Wednesday or Thursday morning on the way to mass why we had to go to church *every* day, when other families only went on Sundays, and some only on holidays, Grandma was clear and fast with her answer. She told me not to worry about what *other* families did, but just what *I* did. I always hated that answer, even though I must admit that I've used it a few times on my own kids.

I admit that that's a parental cop-out, not giving a real answer, but when asked about God, Grandma was right on the mark. She assured me all the time that God was watching over me and knew what I was doing and thinking—not to scare me, but as a way of showing His unconditional love for me.

She used to say all the time, "God is the Sun, Timmy. God is the Sun."

Since I was feeling pretty stupid about not understanding some of the other adult phrases that were thrown around, especially the last rites mix-up, I just let it go. But I did wonder about it at times.

*God is the Sun.* Maybe she meant Jesus. I was taught that he is the "son of God" . . . or did she mean the "sun" in the sky? Who knew? When I asked Grandma to explain it, she told me that she had explained it to my mother, and that when the time was right, my mother would explain it to *me.*

I remember thinking that this was another adult cop-out, but I did eventually get my answer,

and it *did* come from my mom, just as Grandma
Rosie promised.

❋ ❋ ❋

# Chapter Four

## Pictures in a Frame

*It is with bittersweet reflection that I watch the circle of life. As my daughters enjoy a lively birthday, my mother, the woman on whom I have depended my whole life, is slipping away. I find myself already overwhelmed with grief.*

Almost everyone has arrived at the birthday party except for my own parents.

The atmosphere is a-buzz, and everyone is excited to be a part of this celebration, as well as just having the excuse to catch up on all the events in everyone's lives.

In every part of this house—both outside and inside—the energy revolves around familial love. It makes me very happy to be a part of this gathering, as it reminds me of how it felt to grow up here, and I know that Grandma Rosie would be proud. Her wish was that family would always come first— and partying together as a group was especially gratifying for her.

So, our goal this year is not only to celebrate the girls' seventh year, but to make this party extra special for all the guests who will soon find out that this will be my mother's last party with her twin granddaughters.

Even though I'm having these thoughts while Mom's still here, I feel that it's somehow wrong to have them. I find that I've been having a lot of philosophical conversations with myself since we got the diagnosis. *We?* Since *she* got the diagnosis. Sometimes I forget that I'm not the victim here. I sure feel like it, though. Death is worse for those left behind, they say, and it's true.

Strange questions have been running through my mind, such as, *What will I wear at Mom's memorial? What will we dress her in for the viewing? What kind of flowers should I get?* and *Who will come?* I know that this almost macabre way of thinking is just a self-defense mechanism. It's helping me plan and prepare for something that I really can't believe is going to happen. The entire family will be devastated when they find out the news. I say this as if they will be the only ones affected by her physical death and loss. But that's not the case.

My dad, Glenn, will most definitely be in shock. All those years of joking that he's leaving my mom for some buxom blonde type now seems like a scene from an old movie. The reality of their relationship is that Mom *is* Dad's life. I realize that the whole family will have to make a point of really being there for Dad as this progresses. We can't forget that he's been with her longer than we have. He'll be absolutely lost without his beloved wife.

But wait. I have to stop thinking like this. Mom hasn't crossed over *yet*. Sick or not, she's still a vibrant, radiant, energetic woman who always puts everyone ahead of her own well-being. She has dedicated herself to being the best wife, mother, grandmother, aunt, and friend anyone could ask for. As far as I'm concerned, the entire planet as we know it will be different without her energy. Heaven is most definitely getting the better deal.

There are so many errands that I want to run before the party gets into full swing, but it doesn't look as if I'll be able to accomplish them. I'm trying to force myself to get a grip on the events of the day and to be *in the moment.* Relinquishing the role of philosopher seems to be very difficult for me, as I can't stop analyzing and processing and questioning the true meaning of life.

Once again, I realize how good it feels for the house to be filled with the joy and love of family and friends. Melissa and I need this to be the very best party of all, as this celebration will create memories for us all for years to come. Damn! I just realized that I'm not sure if I bought enough film! So many thoughts are crashing through my head that it's a wonder I don't forget to breathe.

That's when the realization hits me. Film? I'm wondering if I have enough film? What will film capture?

Aunt Gina coined a phrase about death after she lost her husband. She'd say, "You die, and then you're nothing but a picture in a frame!"

She would say it often. I wondered at the time why she sounded so cynical about life and death. Didn't she understand what Grandma Rosie taught us? That when we die, we're still connected?

Of course, now that I'm looking down that dark road myself, I can relate to what Aunt Gina meant. Instead of creating cherished memories that will live in my heart for the rest of my life, I'm worried about having enough film.

Also, I've been so preoccupied with my mother's diagnosis and the predicted outcome, that I haven't really been the supportive co-host our family soirée deserves. My eyes just caught Melissa's, and I can tell she that she isn't happy with me today. She keeps shooting me "the look." You know the one I'm referring to. It's the one that doesn't require any verbalization, because its direct, unrelenting glare conveys all that needs to be said. Mel's message at this very moment is: "Do you plan on helping me with all these people, or are you going to daydream all damn day?! It's *your* daughters' party, too, and these are *your* frigging relatives." (Well, maybe I added the profanity myself.)

Usually, after receiving the look, I step up to the plate immediately. But at the moment, my initial reaction is that my wife is being insensitive to my feelings. She should know that my mom's diagnosis is eating me up inside. How can she not understand and be more compassionate?

Deep down, though, I know that this couldn't be further from the truth. Because Melissa lost both her parents early in life, she has a true appreciation of the gift of family. I've known Melissa since our last year of high school, so I know just how deep her pain was when she lost her last surviving parent.

However, my wife is looking forward to this party and reunion for the same reason that I'm dreading it. (There are so many mixed-up, contradictory feelings at a time like this!) She wants to spend as much time as possible with the only Mom she's ever known. And I'm dying inside, knowing that my mother might not be here in a few weeks.

The realization for both of us is that we're losing *our* mom.

❀ ❀ ❀

# Chapter Five

## Treasuring the Day

*As my parents arrive with the girls' new "bundle of joy," I try to reconcile this happy addition to the family with the fact that my mother is saying "good-bye." I vow to pull my family close and to treasure this day.*

The moment I was looking forward to has finally arrived. Mom and Dad are pulling up to the house.

I'm full of excitement and anticipation for so many reasons. On the one hand, I know that Mom doesn't want anyone to know what's going on with her, lest it spoil the day's festivities, but as her son, *I* want to let her know that this is a day to be treasured.

When my parents walk in, I'm surprised and delighted to see that Mom looks like the picture of health. From her head to her toes, she's dressed in a beautiful summer outfit that I'm sure she picked out specifically for today. I don't know whether it's from Saks or Macy's or Bloomingdale's or the boutique downtown, but wherever she bought it, it sure looks good. I realize that I don't have to worry about picking out her clothes for that dreaded day. Knowing my mom, she's already bought a lovely dress, and it's probably sitting in her closet with a note specifying exactly how we should accessorize it.

When the girls see their Gramsy, they fly joyfully into her arms. Dad is standing behind them, watching his wife kneel down and hug his "little petunias," as he calls them. The sentimental look in his eyes brings tears to mine, so I look away. Dad motions for me to step outside with him.

As we walk down the driveway toward my parents' brand-new silver Jeep Cherokee, I can sense that Dad is searching for the words to make today more palatable, but he can't. He is just as new at this as I am.

He speaks slowly, but firmly. "Tim, your mom knows the truth. She doesn't want to discuss treatment options or surgery like the doctor talked about.

She made all her arrangements this morning before we came."

As he speaks, he stares down at the ground, not being able to make eye contact with me. When he finishes, he gazes down the street—the one on which he started his married life. "She doesn't want anyone to know, and she doesn't want anyone to make a big fuss," Dad continues. "She made me promise that only the immediate family will be told at this point. Everyone else can find out afterwards. That's her wish. She doesn't want anyone feeling sorry for her, and she doesn't want them gushing all over her and whispering about her."

Dad pauses before he utters his next statement. He takes a breath and says with a tearful sigh, "She passed out this morning, Tim." With that, Dad's eyes start welling up, and his voice cracks. I think that the stark reality of this is finally hitting him full force.

We're not the type of family that's openly demonstrative and generous with the "I love you's," but in this case, Dad needs a hug, and I need to be the one to give it to him. Although we only stay outside for a few moments, it feels like hours.

I pat Dad on the back, and I tell him that we will all get through this together. He clears his throat, motions toward his new SUV, and says, "I think the present of all presents needs to be walked, Timmy."

With that, we walk over to the Jeep, and Dad pops the rear hatch open. In a small crate in the back, sitting on an old Mickey Mouse towel, is the most beautiful little ball of golden fur. I think it may be the answer to my prayers, the one gift that will help the girls better deal with the pending loss of their grandmother.

When I walk back into the house with this precious gift, I see that my mom and Aunt Gina are deep in conversation over by the window. I don't want to seem intrusive or eavesdrop on their conversation, but it's clear to me that Mom's filling Aunt Gina in on any details she doesn't already know. I still can't believe that the doctor said that in a few weeks or so, she won't be here. She looks fine! How can this be possible?

I see Aunt Gina and my mom embrace for a quick moment, and then they quickly join the rest of the gang sitting in the backyard. I watched the dynamics between them without hearing any of their conversation, but it was so clear to read. Mom was saying good-bye in the best way she could, and her sister was acknowledging it.

As I try to figure out where to hide the puppy so the girls will be surprised later on, I turn around and see Aunt Gina hugging her own daughter, Phyllis. They both look quite upset. This is how news like this spreads. One tells another, and so on. I guess there's no etiquette book that instructs people on how to act when they know a beloved relative is dying. What would Amy Vanderbilt say about that? Is it like the placement of your silverware at the dinner table, or sending out thank-you notes? I don't think there's much of a parallel.

When I turn around, there's my wife, standing in the doorway staring at me.

"What?" I snap.

Melissa just looks at me and smiles faintly. "Nothing," she says, looking directly into my very soul.

"Don't give me that wife psychology where you say nothing, and I know it's something, then I play multiple choice, and then—"

"Tim," she interrupts me, "I love you." She gazes tenderly at me as she says this, and then walks out of the room, back to the endless questions that she's been fielding all day. Here I am thinking that she has no idea what I'm going through, and with three simple words, she lets me know that she understands it all.

I run after her, almost mowing down a group of my cousins who are milling about in the dining room, grab Melissa by the shoulders, and give her a big hug.

"Thank you," I whisper. "Thank you."

❀ ❀ ❀

# Chapter Six

## Songbirds, a Puppy, and Home Movies

*Watching my little birthday songbirds reminds me of a very special gift that they once gave their mother. This memory fills me with hope and reminds me of my Grandma Rosie's unparalleled wisdom. She taught me about "God's Big Plan," which is what I'm musing on now . . .*

After securing our new furry member of the family behind the locked doors of the master bedroom, I once again join the hubbub of the party.

Having spoken with Dad, I feel that our brief moment of shared grief has helped me shake off a little of what I've been carrying around today. It's true that in times like these, if you talk to those around you who are also dealing with the same pain, or who have dealt with something similar in the past, it enables you to move through it better.

Since Mom has arrived, the girls have latched on to their Gramsy and haven't really let her meet and greet the rest of our family and friends beyond waving a simple hello. Mom has been busy playing with her granddaughters' toys, picking flowers in the backyard, inspecting the spot where the girls found a dead bird in the backyard, and watching them model their new swimsuits. My mom is really soaking it all in, not wanting to waste a precious moment. Watching the three of them cavort, I feel a wave of tenderness pass over me. It's a beautiful sight, and I want to etch it indelibly in my mind.

I hear a loud "Hello!" from Melissa, and my consciousness snaps back to the events of the day. As some of the newly arriving guests greet my parents and my girls, I see my mom staring at me. She smiles like she knows what I'm thinking, and we share an unspoken moment of love.

I finally start to mingle with our guests, and Melissa looks relieved that I've started to play the role of host and can help her serve some of the food piling up in the kitchen.

Now that the house is completely filled up with all these different personalities, it's the smell of the day that I notice most. One of the guests has brought in lilac cuttings from her garden, and the delicious scent reminds me that it's my favorite flower, as it always seems to lift my mood.

Now the party is shaping up to be a brilliant success. One of Melissa's talents is definitely her painting, but in the kitchen, she's equally skilled. Everyone loves her signature dish, a dessert called "creampuff swans," which are filled with chocolate pudding, tapioca custard, peanut butter, and more. She's famous for this delicacy, and it's actually created sort of a competition in our family. All the other women have taken up the challenge of coming up with a dessert that will top Melissa's swans. But every year, it's the swans that fly off the dessert table first, pardon the pun.

I think kids have a built-in radar when it comes to certain things, and getting attention is a biggie. Since most of the guests at this moment are more focused on eating than on the girls, the twins realize that the celebration has lost its direction (as far as *they're* concerned), and the grown-ups seem to be ignoring them. My daughter Rachel is the one

45

who brashly alerts the adults, most of whom have mouths full of food: "Attention! Attention! Did you all know that *today is my birthday?*" Then she smiles and curtsies. Everyone explodes in laughter.

Rachel, our first-born (by a few minutes) has always been the ringleader. She's the one who has to be dressed first, wear the best clothes, and Melissa has to make sure that her hair is always perfectly combed. If she doesn't have the prettiest of barrettes in, she isn't happy, and the world will know it.

Rachel's sister, Victoria, is just the opposite. She's basically shy and reserved, and she only feels brave when Rachel is giving her direction. So, Rachel is my little ham. She draws attention to herself every chance she gets. All I know is that they're *both* beautiful, loving little girls, and they will always be my babies—no matter how old they get.

Every year before their party, the girls work for days, preparing a song-and-dance for the crowd. Rachel is the one who forces Victoria to do it with her each year. Enthusiastic (and slightly off-key), they either sing a song that's popular on the radio, or they make one up. I remember the first time they did that. They must have been five years old, and the planning had gone on for days.

Finally, after much rehearsal time between them, the twins had come running into our room yelling, "Mommy! Mommy! We want to sing you a song!"

Melissa beamed at them, and like a child, she made a face at me to flaunt the fact that they were singing for her and not for me. So, behind the girls' backs, I stuck my tongue out at Mel. She laughed.

Melissa sat down on the floor, waiting to be serenaded by her two little songbirds. When the girls started to sing, I watched Melissa's face and was more than surprised. She went from smiling to being perplexed, and then she started to look kind of pale and wan.

> *"Come on, little birdie, come fly with me . . . come on, little birdie, come fly with me.*
>
> *Come on. little birdie, come sit with me . . . come on, little birdie, come sit with me.*
>
> *Come on, little birdie, up in that tree . . . come on, little birdie, up in that tree."*

I found it odd that this song about an innocent little birdie unnerved Melissa, instead of making her chuckle with wonder at the amazing talent of our own Rodgers and Hammerstein duo.

When the girls finished singing their first-ever duet, Melissa did manage to smile, and when she looked up, she seemed younger, somewhat transformed. She asked the girls in wonderment, "Where did you learn that song? Who taught it to you?"

Without skipping a beat, they held each other's hands and jumped up and down in front of Melissa on the floor, yelling: "Jajee Joe! Jajee Joe! Jajee Joe!"

As the words fell from their lips, so did the tears from Melissa's eyes. She looked at me in awe out of the corner of her eyes, and hugged and kissed both girls, offering them her appreciation and praise for their special song. She told them that she loved it and that it was the best song she had ever heard. The girls were ecstatic that they were able to please their mom so much.

Rachel and Victoria ran off to their room to get ready for bed, and Melissa just sat there, looking somewhat stunned. At this point, I was feeling like I was in an episode of *The Twilight Zone* and Rod Serling was going to walk out of my closet at any moment. All I was able to think was, *Did I miss something here?*

Then I very quickly thought that we might have been rapidly approaching that week where chocolate cravings run rampant and Hallmark card commercials make Melissa cry.

Sitting on the floor, looking straight ahead for a moment, she turned her head in my direction. She smiled through her tears and looked lovingly toward me like I had just given her a five-carat diamond— or a great back rub.

I asked her if she wouldn't mind explaining what had just happened.

She proceeded to tell me that *Ja Jee,* or *Dziadek,* to be precise, is the name for "Grandpa" in Polish. Joe was Melissa's father's name, and he used to sing that same exact song about the birdie to Melissa to help her get to "dreamland" when she was just a little girl.

Melissa and I only discussed the incident that one time, and we never brought it up again. You see, we just couldn't explain how the girls would have known about that song, since they had never known their maternal grandfather, and Melissa had never told them about her special song. It unnerved both of us—but in a positive way.

I now believe that the songbird incident was Mel's dad's way of letting her know that even though he had never met his grandchildren, he was still connected. Every now and then, the girls will break out into the birdie song, and Melissa takes it as a sign that her father is still with her.

Today's birthday song by Rachel and Victoria is a take-off of a popular top-40 song, and this is certainly different from watching them sing about a cute little bird. It seems as if they're trying to impersonate go-go dancers, and I think to myself as I watch with raised eyebrows that I should throw out all the TVs in the house—I don't want my little angels growing up too fast.

We are three hours into the party when Melissa decides that we need to get down to the actual cake-cutting and gift-giving ceremony. She gathers all the guests together in the big party room in the back of the house, and "Happy Birthday" is sung, the gifts are opened, and there is much frivolity and cheering all around.

I gaze at Rachel and Victoria, and I'm amazed that these dear children are mine and that they're already turning seven. It seems like just yesterday that we found out that Melissa was pregnant, and then when we learned that we'd be having twins, we were doubly ecstatic. Now they're getting ready to enter the second grade in a week or so.

*"Mommy, Mommy!"* screeches Victoria from down the hall, jolting me out of my reverie. In the middle of all the joyous chaos, she had gotten up to go to the bathroom without anyone even noticing. Rachel and Melissa go flying down the hall toward the master bedroom, and I follow.

"I was walking past your bedroom, and I heard the sound of a baby crying. Mommy, I think there's a crying baby in your room! You have to open the door!" Victoria is very agitated, but Melissa just shoos her and her sister back into the party room.

"Tim?" Melissa is looking at me with her hands on her hips. "I think we need to take care of this sooner, rather than later. I know you wanted to wait until the other kids left, but I think the cat's out of the bag."

"Dog." I reply. "The *dog's* out of the bag, in this case." I laugh at my own joke. Melissa looks at me and rolls her eyes. She tells me to round up the twins and the rest of the parade of children and to meet her in the party room.

I do as she asks, and with everyone gathered around expectantly, we bring out the gyrating box that I've put the puppy in and place it in the middle of the floor. As the kids sit around with wide eyes, wondering what could possibly be in there, it suddenly jerks wildly and falls over onto its side. The cover falls off, and timidly and with great trepidation, a small, golden bundle of fur peeks out. There's a moment of stunned silence.

Jasper, as he's about to be named by my daughters, steps out of the box with his tail hanging low between his hind legs, and his head cowering down. He looks around slowly, and when he sees my mom, a recognizable face, his head perks up and his tail starts to wag. At this point, the kids are starting to laugh and scream, and all the noise scares poor Jasper into a small piddling frenzy. Mom gets down on her hands and knees to comfort the poor little guy as I clean up the mess, and it's at that point that she reveals to my girls that this wonderful ball of love is a present for *them*.

Melissa and I affirm to Rachel and Victoria that, yes, this is their surprise birthday present. We try to tell them about the responsibility attached to having a puppy, but we quickly realize that they're oblivious. All they want to do is scratch Jasper and pet him and love him.

For about ten minutes, all the partygoers watch as the puppy runs from twin to twin, giving them kisses (and a few playful bites) with his little pink tongue. Then the kids go off to the yard to play with their new friend. Throughout the day, we see the girls and their buddies dressing up poor Jasper in Rachel's baby doll dresses, putting him in a carriage, and even wearing sunglasses. It's obvious that he's a hit!

At one point as my parents are watching the kids play, I see my mom and dad exchange a glance, and I can tell that even without speaking, they know exactly what the other is thinking. They're remembering the day that my dad gave my mom Chester, the wonder dog, also known as my brother, protector, and best friend in the entire world. Some kids used to make fun of him, nicknaming him "Chester the Molester," and boy, did that make Mom angry.

I miss him so much! I only hope that the girls' bond with Jasper is as strong as mine was with my best buddy.

As the final gifts are being opened, the kids' end of the party starts to lose its steam, with some of the children taking naps on towels they've laid out on the grass.

The adults congregate in the rec room, and Dad announces that it's time for . . . the dreaded home movies. Before he came over, he secretly went through his entire collection and handpicked various reels of eight-millimeter film that he thought would be fun to revisit.

We all join together, bumping elbows as we position ourselves on various sofas, pillows, and available floor space so that we can prepare to travel back in time.

As soon as the first frame of footage of Grandma Rosie and her beloved son, Clyde, hits the old torn white screen, the entire energy of the room changes, and the mood transforms from buoyant and lively to bittersweet and poignant.

I watch Mom stare into the eyes of her handsome and talented brother on the screen, and at that moment, he starts to sing directly into the camera. The lyrics of the song, coupled with his lilting voice, lift the draining energy in the room, and at that moment, we're all reflecting on those we've loved and lost—and the joy they've brought to our lives, no matter how short or long they've been on this Earth.

As we stare in rapt attention at the movie screen, we take in the sight of all our relatives who are no longer here with us. Uncle Clyde is the first one to pop up, but now there's an endless parade of familiar faces appearing in front of our eyes as if they're still here.

As I look over at my mom, I know that she's wondering if all these faces of yesteryear will be the faces of her tomorrows. Will she see them when she crosses over? Will her loved ones welcome her on the other side, as we all want to believe? I hope so.

Melissa isn't allowing herself to travel down this trip to memory lane. She's still being the consummate hostess of this party, bustling around, procuring food and drinks for the guests. Only the immediate family can really appreciate this "history lesson" anyway.

As Dad puts on another reel, showing me as a young boy at one of my own birthday parties, everyone starts to tease me about how cute I look as I walk across the screen. Everyone tries to guess how old I am, but I know immediately: It's my ninth birthday party. They guess every other age except for that one. I know immediately that I'm not eight because I remember that by the time I turned nine, we had not only lost Uncle Clyde, but Grandma Rosie had also left us, and then one of the most profound traumas that a child my age can go through took place: I lost my dog, Chester.

I find myself time-traveling back, back, back ... blocking out the events of today. I'm no longer just watching a home movie—I'm actually *in* it! I don't question the experience. I just allow myself to participate in this amazing retrospective. . . .

❋ ❋ ❋

# Part II

# Chapter Seven

## Somewhere in Time

*Like ripples on a pond, my memories transport me back in time. I'm reliving and absorbing the experiences that I had as a child.*

*Past my 50s, 40s, 30s, 20s, and teens . . . and now back to the tender age of 8. Yes, I'm a child again, and it's as if I'm right there, in my little-boy body, experiencing everything as a child would. . . . Didn't it all just happen a minute ago. . . .*

I'm eight years old, preparing to turn nine next week. We're going to be having a big party for my birthday, and I'm pretty much looking forward to it. However, the one thing I know I'm *not* looking forward to is having to deal with my cousin, Steve. He is the most obnoxious member of my family. He has this way of drawing all the attention to him in every situation. It's always all about Steve. Last year, he started to scream and cry just because *his* name wasn't on the cake along with mine. I mean, it wasn't *his* birthday—why would *his* name be on the cake?!

I had a long talk with my Dad about that incident, and he promised me that Steve's name wouldn't be on my cake this year either. We'll see if he acts up again. A year ago, I was fortunate to get what mommy refers to as a "love tap" on the back of my head. Why? Well, let's just say that I started laughing at Steve and calling him a whining little baby when he started having his tantrum, and that made it worse. It kind of shocked me that my mom hit me, or "love-tapped" me. It didn't hurt or anything, but it was embarrassing for me to be reprimanded in front of my bratty cousin.

Even though it's not my birthday yet, and Steve isn't even here, he's already in the spotlight. But it's not his fault, so I'm going to let him slide. Let's just stay that he's had a really bad year. The worst. His dad, my Uncle Clyde, was killed in a car accident several months ago. It was a head-on collision, and there were no survivors. Steve's mom, Aunt Marsha, hasn't been the same since. Grandma Rosie helps to take care of them both now.

My Uncle Clyde was the coolest man on this planet (besides my dad, of course). He was what everyone would call a ray of sunshine (how did his son turn out so different?). Anyway, some of his friends even called him "Sonny" for that reason. He was on his way to becoming famous, everyone used to say. He had the gift of song. When he sang, people would stop and listen in awe.

Mommy once told me that the family was driving to Brooklyn to have dinner one night, and Uncle Clyde was singing in the back seat with the windows down. The couple in the next car started to clap at the red light. That kind of thing happened all the time.

When he was young, Uncle Clyde's vocal teacher even made a special trip to our house to tell Grandma Rosie that her son was going to be the next Frank Sinatra. I don't know if Uncle Clyde really wanted to be the next *anything*, as he was more involved in the business aspect of promoting singers in cabaret clubs in New York City. But it sure was flattering for him to hear.

Uncle Clyde would only sing occasionally to open up for the acts he promoted, but Mommy said that the patrons would keep shouting for him to sing another and another. Sometimes the people in the other acts took offense, and I know that that frustrated Uncle Clyde to no end. I overheard him tell Grandma Rosie once that he only wanted to sing for his mama. When his father, my Grandpa Jack, died, Uncle Clyde would sing to Grandma Rosie, since it was the only thing that seemed to make her feel better.

When Grandpa Jack was still alive, he and my grandmother had a favorite song, and Uncle Clyde always sang it for them. It was "You Are Always Here with Me"—a wartime classic that has been sung in a lot of languages. Uncle Clyde would sing it in both Italian and English. Now that Grandpa is gone, it has even more meaning for Grandma Rosie. She gazes at her late husband's picture and sings that song to him, letting him know that he's always in her heart.

I once asked her about getting married again, and she laughed. She told me that she'd had it good, and she didn't *want* or *need* another husband. She was complete.

So, you can see why Steve is almost *deserving* of the spotlight at this time. Everyone's feeling sorry for him since his dad was killed. I understand. He's just a little kid, after all.

I'm really going to try and be considerate of his feelings next week. Maybe I'll even let him help me blow out my candles or open a few presents. It must be hard losing a parent.

What about Grandma Rosie, though? She lost her only son, and he was her youngest, her baby.

I know that it was incredibly painful for Grandma. She cried and yelled at the funeral parlor when it was time to go to the cemetery. My daddy and Uncle Dom had to carry her out of the room in the chair that she was sitting in. She just wouldn't leave. She wanted that moment in time to stand still.

What amazed me the most was how she dealt with Uncle Clyde's death after the burial. Everyone thought that she was going to need to see a doctor and get some tranquilizers or something. That was what everyone was whispering behind her back. But she was stronger than they all gave her credit for.

I was taught in school that taking pills is bad for you unless you really need them, so I didn't want Grandma Rosie to do anything that could hurt her. I ran to her and told her that I was afraid that Mommy and Aunt Gina were going to force her to take pills before the special memorial that the people in Uncle Clyde's business were having for him. I explained to her that I was upset about this and didn't want her to get in trouble and do drugs. Grandma Rosie just smiled at me fondly, touched my hair, and hugged me.

I was really excited about being allowed to go all the way into New York City for Uncle Clyde's special memorial. Mommy explained that this would be different from what we did right after he died— going to church and the cemetery and all. That was really sad. Mom said that Uncle Clyde's best friend in life, Patrick, who had known him since he was four years old, had organized this tribute. Those two were as close as twin brothers, and Patrick wanted to celebrate his late friend's life.

When we walked into the small church on the Upper West Side of Manhattan, I saw all these people I didn't know, but they all knew my Uncle Clyde. I remember everyone whispering about all the celebrities who were in the audience. I didn't know any of them, but they must have been very famous and important, and I was really impressed that they loved my uncle so much.

Each person got up and expressed their condolences to Aunt Marsha, my cousin Steve, and Grandma Rosie. They each acknowledged how important Uncle Clyde's family had been to him, and how he had constantly referred to them when speaking with both business and personal acquaintances.

The basic theme to Uncle Clyde's life was love. It seemed that he learned on Earth what we assume that only people in Heaven know. Basically, he understood and lived the definition of unconditional love. One by one, Uncle Clyde's friends told stories about how he had touched their lives in some way or helped them through a difficult time. They expressed gratitude for his friendship, and a lot of them mentioned that Uncle Clyde always took the time to keep in contact with his friends, no matter how busy he was. They said that he had the gift of always being able to say the right thing at the right time. He never asked for anything in return, but simply gave his love out unconditionally, and he knew how to make each and every person he was close to feel special.

After Uncle Clyde's friends had paid tribute to him, I was shocked to see my mom stand up in front of all those people. She composed her thoughts, and then told a story about the time that she and Clyde had gone to the local mall to buy a gift for their sister, Gina.

Mommy began, "Every year when it was one of our birthdays, the other two siblings would go shopping together for a nice present. Well, this one afternoon, we decided to buy Gina a smart wool jacket. Being that Clyde was in show business, he seemed to have a knack for picking out just the right thing when it came to fashion.

"Now, as you know, Clyde had so much charisma that it should have been bottled, and he attracted people wherever he went. Well, this day was no different. The combination of his handsome face and his positive energy just seemed to draw people to him.

"Anyway, Gina and I are the same size, so while I was trying on one of the jackets in this one store, the salesgirl came over, and Clyde struck up a conversation with her about the cut of the jacket. He was remarking on how the lines made my waist look small, and the padding in the shoulders was flattering, too."

Mommy cleared her throat to continue.

"The jacket was sold and shouldn't have been out on the floor, so Clyde talked the salesgirl into ordering another one for us from a satellite store. Even though that wasn't the store's policy, Clyde explained that it was a gift for his sister, and the salesgirl would simply have to make an exception.

"Who was going to argue with that face and smile? Unfortunately, a few days later, Clyde had his accident. One of the most difficult things that I've ever had to do was to go back to that store. I walked in and quietly handed that same salesgirl the claim ticket to pick up the jacket, and when she asked for Clyde, I told her about the accident. This stranger, who had only met him once, immediately burst into tears. He really touched everyone he met."

After my mom had finished telling her story, the most incredible thing happened. A famous Broadway actress, singer, and dancer named Victoria Regan slowly made her way down the aisle toward the front of the church. Mommy and Aunt Gina were so impressed that someone of her stature would take the time to be here for Uncle Clyde. Mommy told Aunt Gina that they had known each other for years.

Victoria walked behind the podium, which was covered with the most beautiful tiny pink roses. She composed herself and smiled. I remember the way the light reflected off her fiery-red hair and alabaster complexion, and how she just seemed to "look" famous, even though, at the time, I didn't even know what she was famous for.

She looked around at all the faces in the room and spoke with great emotion. "It is unfortunate that we are all brought together at an event such as this one, to memorialize someone whom we all loved. This man who is responsible for bringing people from all walks of life together was a special person, a gift to us all. Our world is a darker place without the light of his soul to illuminate it."

Victoria closed her eyes, took a deep breath, and smiled. When she opened her blue eyes, she looked straight ahead as if she were addressing someone standing in front of her. Her words flowed with ease: "A few short years ago, I had the opportunity to meet a man who changed my views on death. His name is not important, but his work *is*. He is a psychic medium who has the ability to communicate with those who have crossed over. Now I know that there are those of you who may find this difficult to believe, but I know that this is valid and real. I know that death is not final. It is not the end that I once thought it was . . . and because of that, I'm not going to stand here and talk about how great Clyde *once was*. No. Instead, I'm going to take this opportunity to tell him directly how I feel.

"Clyde, I know you're here, I know you wouldn't miss a party like this. . . ." Everyone burst into laughter.

As Victoria Regan continued to speak to her beloved friend, the people in the audience laughed and cried and even shared tissues with each other. As the tears streamed down her face, she proceeded to tell Clyde how much she loved and appreciated him, and she thanked him for being such a driving force in her life and career. Even though he was substantially younger than she was, he always took care of her like a father would. She made sure to thank Marsha for sharing Clyde with the world, and she told Steve how lucky he was to be able to say that Clyde was his dad.

After Victoria had completely expressed everything in her heart and soul that she wanted to relay to Clyde, she looked out over the room and said to the audience, "I must honor a request that Clyde once made of me. Clyde, I know that I promised you

I would do this, but you will have to give me the energy and strength to be able to complete it."

With that, she explained that after one of her many opening nights, she was asked to sing at a memorial service for a fellow singer who had passed. She had told Clyde that she felt awkward about it, and he told her that he would go with her and stand in the back of the room, and that she should imagine that she was singing to him. They got into a conversation about death and dying, and somehow Clyde made her promise that she would sing at his memorial, with a special provision attached.

Even though Victoria knew at the time that it would be difficult for her to honor Clyde's request, she had promised him she would, and now was the time for her to keep her promise. At that point, Victoria's accompanist joined her on stage and sat at the upright piano to her right.

Victoria looked down at Grandma Rosie. "Rose? I know that this may be difficult, but Clyde made me promise that if anything ever happened to him, that I would sing this song for you.

Please know that it is for you and him that I sing . . ."

The music began, and it was clear what Uncle Clyde's request was. The melody for "You Are Always Here with Me" began, and Mommy and Aunt Gina gasped. Grandma Rosie's eyes opened wide, brimming over with the emotion that only a mother could feel for a child whom she has out-lived.

Victoria began:

*"You are always here with me*
*you're in my heart and in my mind,*
*you're in my reverie . . ."*

Grandma Rosie immediately stood up. Aunt Gina grabbed her arm to make sure that she was all right, but she was fine. She was standing in honor of her son. She was standing in honor of the unbreakable bond that they would always share.

*"All my dreams and thoughts are all of you*
*All the memories we made, our whole life*
*through . . .*

*"When we are apart,*
*I'm part of you*
*You're part of me*

*Always know our love will last right
through eternity, for you will always be a
part of me . . ."*

As Victoria sang with as much emotion and
feeling as she could, Grandma Rosie made her way
toward the front of the church.

*"Know that when we have to part
Just always keep me in your heart
Close your eyes and I'll be there
You wait and see . . .*

*"I'll be the sun that warms your heart
I'll be the stars that show the way
I'll be a gentle breeze to blow around
you every day . . ."*

Everyone was mesmerized as Grandma Rosie
passed by their particular row. Grandma stopped in
the exact location in which Victoria had been staring when she was addressing Clyde. I wondered if
they were somehow seeing him. I wanted to see
him, too.

*"I can never go away,*
*the memories made are here to stay*
*and I'll be here with you forever and a day . . .*

*"Please know that I am always there,*
*and our love is everywhere*
*Just close your eyes, reach out for me,*
*and I'll be there when a love is meant to be*
*It goes on past eternity,*
*and so my love for you . . . will always be.*
*You are always here with me. . . ."*

As Victoria held the last note of the song, she opened her eyes and saw Grandma Rosie directly in front of her. With the accompanist still playing the song's final notes, Victoria ran down the three short steps of the stage into the embrace of Clyde's mom, my Grandma. It was then that the entire room burst into applause that seemed to go on forever. It was clear that they weren't just applauding Victoria's angelic voice; they were applauding life—and love.

When the clapping died down, Victoria started to escort Grandma Rosie to her seat, but instead, Grandma proceeded to walk up the three steps to the stage. As she pulled the microphone to her face, there was complete silence in the room. You could only hear a few sniffles emanating from some of the guests.

Grandma Rosie spoke slowly and deliberately. She didn't seem the least bit intimidated to be standing in front of an audience of professional speakers, singers, and actresses. She only spoke for a moment, but that was all she needed.

"I, too, don't believe that death is the end," Grandma Rosie began. "I believe it is just an invitation to the family reunion we will all have one day. I only asked one thing from my Clyde when I got the news. I asked him to let me know that he is in Heaven with his father. I needed him to tell me in some way that he was with my Jackie.

"Thank you, Victoria. I now know that it is true. 'You Are Always Here with Me' is a song that defined the love my husband and I had for each other, and Clyde always sang it for both of us. At this time, I will tell him for all of us here today: Clyde . . . you will always be in our hearts. Thank you all for loving my son."

When she had finished speaking, the audience didn't know whether to applaud or just sit and wait for someone else to take the stage. Grandma Rosie didn't cry at all, but simply pulled one of the pink roses off the podium and smelled it as she walked down the aisle, passing by all of us—my parents, Aunt Gina, Uncle Dom, Aunt Marsha, Steve, and me.

She walked out of the church and waited outside for all of us to join her. I couldn't understand why nobody was going after her, so I ran as fast as I could down the aisle. I knew that Grandma Rosie needed a hug. As Uncle Clyde's friend Patrick once again took the podium to thank everyone for coming, I was outside, wrapping my arms around my grandmother.

I looked at her and blurted out, "Grandma, I bet Uncle Clyde is right here, and I bet he's really, really proud of you!"

With tears streaming down her face, she squeezed me tight to her. "I bet he is, too, Timmy. I just bet he is."

❀ ❀ ❀

# Chapter Eight

## Best Friends Forever

*As I continue living through the movie
in my mind, I can't help but think of another
of the loved ones who has touched my life—
my very best friend in the whole world—
my dog, Chester—who passed away when
I was just eight years old.*

Chester was the golden retriever my dad gave
my mom as a Christmas present one year. As
soon as I was born, it was clear that Chester would
be my older brother, protector, and the best friend
anyone could ever ask for. He was only four years
older than I was, and we grew up together.

My sweet Chester licked me to sleep every single night, and he woke me up for school every

morning. Daddy told me that Chester slept right next to me from the day I was born. If I was asleep in the crib, Chester was sleeping on the floor beside me. He was clearly my guardian. One time when I was a baby, a neighbor came to see me, but Chester didn't recognize her. Now I don't actually *remember* this, but it has been recounted to me on numerous occasions. Chester barked and barked, corralling her away from me in the crib, and he wouldn't stop until my mom came into the room to let him know that everything was all right.

Chester's favorite pastime was running. The faster Chester could run, the happier he would be. On special days, I was allowed to take Chester up to the schoolyard field behind our house. All you would see was this streak of gold running low to the ground, in circles and straight lines. He knew that running on the field was a special treat, so when we were allowed to go there, he just had the best time. My parents were afraid that he would get too crazy running around and I wouldn't be able to control him and he'd run away. But I knew that would never happen. He would never leave me. He was my pal, my other half.

Mrs. Silvia, the teacher of my religion class, taught us that we all have guardian angels watching over us. One day she asked her students if we had ever seen ours. I immediately responded that not only did I *see* mine, but I played with him every day. The teacher looked at me with confusion and asked who I thought my angel *was*. I told her and the class that my guardian angel was Chester, my dog. Everybody laughed at me for believing that a dog could be my angel. I know that Mrs. Silvia felt sad for me when the other kids were laughing. But what did they know? I knew that what I said was true.

Some of my friends were jealous of the relationship that Chester and I shared. We actually had the ability to know what the other was thinking. Chester knew that he had to behave in the house and on the field when I was with him. He also knew that running wasn't allowed in the house—he was too big. Indoors, instead of running around, we would play army games. I would send out the troops, placing one of his many plastic squeak toys somewhere in the house. I wouldn't tell him which one to go and fetch, but I would *think* it really hard. Almost every time, he would retrieve the right toy. When I would tell my friends about these incidents, they would scoff, "Oh, it's just a coincidence," but I knew better.

There were times when Chester would be lying on the bed, and I would "feel" as if I knew what he needed or wanted. So, if *I* felt that I knew what *he* wanted, whether it was water, food, or to go outside, why wouldn't he know the same about *me?*

I stopped trying to convince everyone that we had a special bond. I don't think that I had any special powers like Dr. Doolittle, but I just *knew* Chester. I knew everything that he really loved (besides me), and one of those things was . . . being massaged! Yes, massaged.

When we would return from one of our running "field trips," I would sit on the couch and yell out, "Chester! Want a massage?"

No matter where in the house he was, or how tired he might have been, Chester *always* wanted a massage. He would lay his body across my lap, and I would first scratch him all over, and then I would slowly and methodically massage all of Chester's tired muscles.

— ❀ —

Hearing my own voice yell out, "Chester, want a massage?" from the rec room where the old home movies are still being watched, brings me back to the present.

I hear a familiar bark call out to me. I manage to eke out a melancholy smile at the sight of my sweet dog. I think to myself, *If Chester were here today, this cancer thing would be more bearable. He would help me deal with it.* I look at the screen and see an unsuspecting, innocent, eight-year-old Timothy hanging all over his Chester. I want to scream out to the little boy sitting there in the backyard of the home where I'm living today, and time-travel back to him.

And what would I tell him? I would tell him to prepare himself well for the times ahead. As he turns nine, he will learn a lot about the meaning of life and death, and most important, he will get to ask his mom what Grandma Rosie actually meant when she'd enigmatically ask: "What if God were the Sun?"

❋ ❋ ❋

# Chapter Nine

## What If God Were the Sun?

*I find revisiting my childhood very help-
ful. The lessons of the past fill my present
with some solace. When I was eight, my
family lost Uncle Clyde, Grandma Rosie,
and Chester. But now, important things are
starting to happen, and I finally find out
about God smiling down on me like the sun.
Yes, this will be a pivotal birthday, indeed.
This year, my ninth, I'll receive some of my
most priceless gifts ever.*

The big day is just about here. Tomorrow is my
ninth birthday, and I can hardly wait for the
celebration to begin. It's all I can think about. All

my friends from school will be here, and all the kids from the neighborhood are coming over to engage in the usual ritual of eating cake, playing games, and bringing gifts. The most exciting thing about having a birthday so close to Halloween is that the assortment of candy available in the stores at this time of year is absolutely the best. I think it's even better than at Easter!

I think that for most kids, the most enjoyable part of having a party is opening the presents. You never know who's going to bring you the best gift. The hard part is being excited when someone gives you something as dopey as money, or even worse, clothes. Do you know how hard it is to fake excitement over clothes?

Yeah, I just love the gift part. I don't care what's really inside the box; I just love the ritual of shaking it and trying to guess what's inside. I know, it's better to give than to receive. Well, that's true every day of the year except your own birthday!

Whenever I'm about to celebrate another birthday, I always think about the time of day I was born: 9:15 A.M. on the nose. Every year up until I started school, Mom would come into my room and wake me up at that time with three distinct kisses—one kiss on each cheek, and then one on my forehead.

When I began kindergarten at the age of five, we had to be at school at eight o'clock in the morning, sharp. But, believe it or not, Mom never failed me. She would find out which classroom I was in, she'd drive her car around to that side of the building, and at precisely 9:15, she would honk her horn three times. Beep! Beep! Beep! In my mind, I could imagine her kissing my two cheeks and my forehead. I didn't dare tell anyone. I don't even think my dad knew about this. It was something special between us. (Not to mention that I didn't want anyone making fun of me.)

This year, my birthday falls on a Saturday. And I have no doubt that I will wake up to my mother's kisses. Even if I happen to *wake* up earlier than 9:15, I'm not going to *get* up before then, just so my mom and I can continue this tradition. We both really look forward to it.

The day has just sped along, and it's now the Friday evening before my birthday party. I'm counting down the minutes. As I start getting ready for bed, I almost begin the nightly ritual of taking Chester outside one last time before we can curl up together. But then the realization hits me: Chester's gone, too. At this point, my eyes begin to well up with stinging tears. This will be the first birthday without my best friend in the whole world.

I'm thinking that we're going to have to work really hard to make sure no one gets too sad at my birthday party. After all, we lost so many loved ones over the last year. First, it was Uncle Clyde; then seven months later, Grandma Rosie. She had cancer, but she died in her sleep, and the doctor said that that was the most peaceful way for her to go.

But I overheard Mommy telling Daddy that she died of a broken heart. She just missed Grandpa Jack and Uncle Clyde so much. Aunt Gina told Mommy that this was the worst year our family has seen in years. We lost so many people in such a short period of time. And although Chester wasn't a person, I miss him just as much.

I try to go to the bathroom, but the door is shut, and I can hear my mom crying. She's been doing that for the last few months. I hate to see or hear her cry. It makes me want to fix it, but I don't know how. I feel like I need to do *something*, though, so I bang really hard on the bathroom door, disturbing her private moment, yelling, "I gotta go . . . hurry up! I gotta go!"

"Tim, go to your room, and I'll be out in a minute. Okay, honey?" Mom responds.

When she comes out, it's clear to me that she's definitely been crying. She comes into my room and tells me that we need to talk. Her tone is serious and intense—way too serious for someone planning on celebrating such a phenomenal thing as me turning nine. She tells me to go and brush my teeth and come back and put on my pajamas, and she'll come back in after I'm done so that we can talk.

I think it may be her tone of voice, but I can feel my energy and mood changing. Suddenly I'm not feeling as good about my party and all the planned festivities.

After I brush my teeth, I put on my pajamas and climb into bed. As I'm lying there waiting for my mom to come in and talk with me, I start to wonder if I'm in trouble, but I can't think of anything I've done wrong. Then when I explore every possible thing that I might have done and can't come up with anything, I start getting really nervous.

My friend Ricky's mom had a talk with him recently. His mother wanted to tell Ricky that she and his father were getting a divorce. No, it *can't* be that. Just the idea of Mom and Dad not being married to each other is impossible, so I dismiss that thought entirely.

Waiting for Mom to come in, I start thinking about tomorrow's party again. I mostly think about who will be there, and then I start getting really sad. I know why I'm feeling like this. And now I have an idea what Mommy wants to talk about. I look over at the three pictures in a frame sitting on my windowsill: Grandma Rosie, Uncle Clyde, and Chester. That's probably why Mom was crying in the bathroom.

Mom is entering my room now, and she seems to be on a mission. First, the dreaded "Did you brush your teeth?" or "toofies," as she prefers to call them. I don't know where or when she started on that word, but I just pray that she won't ever use it around one of my friends. I would never live down a word like that. I've tried repeatedly to make her stop saying it, but she just laughs and says it anyway.

"I'm not a little boy anymore," I always tell her with exasperation, just as I do tonight.

"You will *always* be my little boy," she says, "so hush up and say your prayers. Your party will be here before you know it."

She hesitates. "You're excited about tomorrow, aren't you, Tim?" she asks as she pulls up my favorite Spiderman blanket.

"I guess."

"What do you mean?" Mom looks at me with a puzzled expression on her face. "Everyone you invited is coming, and that should make you happy, right?"

I think to myself that *everyone* isn't the word that we should be using to define the guest list for tomorrow's party. *Everyone* doesn't include Grandma Rosie, Uncle Clyde, or Chester.

Instead of Mom trying to find the right words to bring up what she wants to talk to me about, I decide to seize the moment and say something first.

"Mom, why did Grandma Rosie die?" I ask her abruptly.

Mom just looks at me, clearly taken aback. She was obviously sitting there trying to figure out how to open a conversation about death, and here I went and started it for her.

"Well, Timmy, Grandma Rosie was old, and sometimes older people are just too tired to live, and—"

I interrupt her. "But I heard you say that she died of a broken heart, because she missed Uncle Clyde so much." As I'm saying this, my voice starts to crack, and I can feel my eyes start to water up. "Does this mean that *I* might die, too . . . because I miss Chester so much?"

As I'm rubbing my eyes, Mom slowly sits down on the edge of my bed. I know that she wants to talk about all this, but now I'm thinking that she might be regretting the idea.

After a moment, she breaks into a nervous laugh and answers me. "You're not going to die, Tim. Not now. One day, yes, but not now. But it's something we can't control. It's all a part of God's plan. Grandma Rosie needed to be in Heaven with the rest of our family."

"Including Chester!" I quickly add.

"Yes, Chester, too," she agrees.

Losing three loved ones in less than a year has been difficult for the entire family. Grandma Rosie always said that June was a bad month. It seems kind of weird to me that she would pick one month and badmouth it, but maybe she knew something I didn't.

Mommy would say that Grandma Rosie felt that way because she lost a few of her brothers and sisters in that month. Until this year, I didn't realize that when you *lost* someone it meant that they died. Hearing adults say that someone was "lost," or watching a television show where the doctors would say, "We lost him," has always confused me. I always wondered if one day we would "find" all these people who were "lost" and just have a big "We found them all!" party.

I understand now what it means, though, but I like my meaning better. I like the idea that they're lost or misplaced, because then we *do* have the opportunity to find them again. But now it just seems so sad. I miss them so much. I miss my handsome Uncle Clyde and the special way Grandma Rosie used to hug me . . . and I will never stop missing my Chester. Never, ever.

At this point, I almost start to cry again, and I wonder if Chester got to go to Heaven like Grandma Rosie and Uncle Clyde. All our relatives that die go to Heaven, or at least that's what Mommy once told me. I have to wonder if they let Chester into Heaven, and if so, I wonder who up there will take the time to give Chester a massage.

"Tim? Earth to Timmy . . . come in Timmy." Mom has obviously been trying to capture my attention for the last few minutes. Her tone of voice is more upbeat now, though. I think that my serious adult questions have thrown her a bit, and she's trying to lighten things up. Well, I'm not about to stop now. I need answers.

"You okay, my little man? I know that the last few months have been difficult, to say the least, but tomorrow is almost here, and it's a big day. Your dad and I are worried about you. We want you to enjoy your day. We don't want you to be sad tomorrow."

"Mom . . . I *miss* them!" I look away as I say this so I won't have to see the pained expression on her face. The last thing I want to do is make her cry again tonight.

"I know, Timmy. I know. So do I . . ." She sighs heavily.

Mom suddenly changes the subject and asks me what type of cake I want tomorrow. My choices are the store-bought ice cream cake with the chocolate-covered sprinkles, or the home-baked yellow cake with chocolate icing. I quickly decide on the ice cream cake, but I don't want her to change the subject.

"Mommy, do you believe that we'll ever see them again? In Heaven, I mean."

"Absolutely, Tim. Absolutely," Mommy responds, patting me on the leg. She answers me fast, and I immediately know she's telling me the truth.

I quickly think to myself, *I wonder if this is a good time to tell her about the dream I had with all of them in it. Will she think I'm making it up? Will it upset her?*

My tongue decides to think for me. "Mom, do you believe that we can see them in our dreams?"

"Why?" she asks warily.

That isn't the answer I was expecting. I want the answer to my question, not another question.

"Have you dreamed about Grandma and Clyde and Chester, Timmy?" she asks with hope in her voice. "If you have, then you've received a gift from God."

"Yes, Mommy, I have," I say quietly.

"That's wonderful and special, Timmy. See that—God gave you an early birthday present." Mom says this with so much strength and happiness in her voice that I believe she really means it.

Well, it's true. The other night, I had a dream about all of them, and it felt so real that I woke up crying. Ultimately, though, it was a happy dream, because I was able to hug and play with all of my family that was "lost"—including Chester. I dreamed that Uncle Clyde and Chester were with Grandma Rosie and Grandpa Jack.

Wow! The impact of this is really hitting me now. *I received a gift from God.* Mommy has always told me that all our loved ones are in Heaven with

God. Maybe my dream was His way of letting me know that He's taking good care of them. Well, I hope that God is feeding Chester and letting him run around in Heaven. I mean, besides me, that's what he loved most!

How do I know that Mommy's just not trying to make me feel better, though? I start having doubts. Then I remember my religion teacher, Mrs. Silvia. She once told the class the same thing—that when our friends and family members leave us here, their spirit is greeted by one of God's angels, and their soul goes home.

In class, Mrs. Silvia always talked about God, and what Heaven was like, and how we all have angels. She spoke of it like it was a place that she once visited on a really exciting vacation. She's a great lady who has always answered all our questions, no matter how crazy the other kids in the class think the question is. Come to think of it, she didn't even laugh when I said that I believed that Chester was my guardian angel. She told us that if we had a question, God wanted us to have the answer and we should ask it—no matter what.

"Tim? Is something bothering you?" Mom once again interrupts my reverie. She knows immediately that Chester is on my mind. "You know that

Chester will be with you tomorrow. He wouldn't miss an opportunity to celebrate your birthday."

She says it like it's a fact, and Mom never lies to me. *Can it be true?* I wonder.

Mom continues, "They will all be here tomorrow: Grandpa Jack, Grandma Rosie, Uncle Clyde, and Chester . . . they will all be with you in spirit."

My feelings of missing Chester are so strong that my eyes fill with tears again. I blink a lot, hoping that Mommy won't notice them, but it doesn't work. I have all these tough questions running through my mind. I know that I need them answered right away, and I won't be seeing Mrs. Silvia for another few days.

"Timothy, those tears are nothing to be embarrassed about. Don't hide them. Let them flow. They are a tribute to the memory and love you have for all those we've lost in our lives. It's brave to show your feelings to yourself and the world. So, don't worry, honey. Everybody you love is in Heaven now. How many times have I told you that?" she asks with a lilt in her voice. Then she starts to fold the clothes that I left on the floor.

"Then why do you only cry in the bathroom?" I ask sharply.

"Tim, trust me, I don't *only* cry in the bathroom. I cry in the car, at work, in bed, and anytime some special memory comes into my mind. It's like a wave that washes onto the shore. The tide brings in the memory and soaks the shore . . . and it absorbs the water. Our memories are the waves, and we are the shore. When we cry, we release the negative part of the memory and pay tribute to it. The sad part is pulled out to sea . . . out of you. . . ." Mom looks at me with determination. She wants me to have these answers just as much as I want to hear them.

"So, it's okay to cry?" I ask.

"Don't be silly. Of course it is."

"Then why do you always tell me not to cry when you punish me for doing something wrong? Sometimes you tell me that you'll *give* me something to cry about?" I put forth boldly.

"Tim, that's a different story! Now you're trying to compare apples and oranges. The type of crying I'm referring to is more of a release and a natural reaction to our emotions. Tim, even your father cries!" Mom looks me straight in the eyes to make sure I really hear what she's saying.

"What?! Dad cries?" I ask in shock and disbelief.

"Tim, your father cries during commercials. Are you kidding?" She chuckles as she says this.

"Does Chester know when I cry for him? Does it make him sad?" I ask.

Mom replies, "No, honey. He knows that you're dealing with one of God's gifts, and that it's something you need to take the time to do. It's part of the grieving process that everyone has to go through. I bet that Chester is right up there in Heaven helping you get through this. I believe Grandma Rosie, Uncle Clyde, and Grandpa Jack are with us, too, loving us and helping us from Heaven.

"Timmy, when you love someone, you learn to count on that love always being there. Sometimes we don't appreciate the fact that it *won't* always be there. When a person dies, they're no longer with us to touch and hold. So, the gift of grief is God's way of dealing with the love we have for the person who has died. Many people think grief is a bad thing, but it isn't. Grief is a way to explore the depth of our feelings and emotions for a person who won't be in our lives in the way that we're used to having them. Think of grief as a placeholder for love, a reminder to us all that we're capable of feeling such a strong emotion. Grief is the other side of love, Timmy."

"Like the love I feel for Chester!" I exclaim.

"That's right. You love Chester, so missing him and crying about him is your way of exploring the gift of love that God gave the two of you. So remember when you're going through these feelings— what we often call the grief process—that it's God's way of helping you explore the love you feel."

*Wow! She's really talking to me like an adult.* I understand most of what she's telling me, but a part of me feels that I'm still not getting it all, so I blurt out my next question.

"Mom, is there *really* a God?" I ask with a tremor in my voice, afraid of Mom's—and God's— reaction to my question.

Mom responds without blinking an eye. "Of course there's a God, Timothy. Weren't you paying attention to what I just said?"

Now, feeling brave, I decide to go for all the questions I have so that I can get a good night's sleep and be ready for the party tomorrow.

"You say that the people we love who leave us go to Heaven to be with God. But where is it? How do I get there?"

I'm posing my questions so fast that I have to gasp for breath.

Mom sits down on the end of my bed and smiles at me with her big green eyes, preparing to patiently answer all my queries. "This is how it works, honey. God helped you pick out who would be your family on Earth to love and teach you all the lessons that your soul needed to learn. He then sent you to us out of His love. The job for us was to love and protect you here on Earth like He does for all of us from Heaven."

With a doubtful expression, I respond, "Really, Mom?"

"Yes. Have I ever lied to you? No, I never have, and I won't begin to now. Grandpa Jack went to Heaven first, and then when it was time for Grandma to leave us and go to Heaven, Grandpa came and met her." She went on as happy tears formed in her eyes. "When Grandma Rosie left us, she saw Grandpa Jack and Uncle Clyde in her bedroom the night before. She told us that they were there to escort her home. We thought that maybe she was dreaming, but the next night, Grandma Rosie died in her sleep, with a smile on her face."

This news makes me very happy.

"I can't help but wonder if the same thing happened to Chester. Would Chester's dog family have come to meet him, or would Grandma Rosie have been there? We all knew that she was afraid of Chester and would chase him with a broom. He loved to tease her. Maybe he was met by Uncle Clyde. I don't know. But I hope they'll all be there for my party tomorrow."

Mom starts to laugh. "I'm positive that they're all together and will be with us tomorrow. Chester, especially. He wouldn't miss a chance to see you happy, not to mention all the cake that might fall on the floor."

Now, with much lighter energy, Mom tells me to get some sleep.

Get some sleep? I'm on a roll here. I'm not done yet. I need more answers. Now might be the perfect time to ask what Grandma Rosie meant when she talked about God being the Sun. I decide that I just have to ask.

"But Mom, there's more. Where's Heaven?" I throw this out at her just as she's getting up from the bed to shut off the light and go to bed herself.

Stopping for a moment, Mom looks past me at the picture of Grandma Rosie on my wall from two summers ago. She smiles faintly, and then tells me that she will share the explanation that Grandma gave her when she was about my age and needed answers to these same questions.

Now I'm getting excited. I feel like I'm learning the family secrets.

Mom explains: "Grandma taught us that we're all a glass of water. Every person is a glass of water on a counter in God's home, known as Heaven. Whether the glass is tall, short, fat, thin, black, or white, we are all special and unique in our own way. When we're born, we are that empty glass. God pours our soul, our spirit, into our glass. And we live out the rest of our lives as that glass of water. Over time, the water—our soul—changes form."

"You mean we *evaporate?*" I interject with a word from science class.

"Well, it's sort of like that, Tim. You see, when a person dies, the soul leaves the glass, very much like the water evaporates; it joins the air. The way a caterpillar becomes a butterfly, our spirit becomes as light as the breeze . . . surrounding and caressing those we've left behind. So you see, Tim, Heaven and our loved ones are *all* around us. *Heaven is all around us.* Like the air." Mom smiles as I nod in understanding.

Mom kisses me goodnight, and then leans in and says, "I'm so glad that you're asking these questions. My little man is really growing up."

"So God is a really cool guy then, right?" I ask.

"I think God would like you to think of Him as a really cool guy. As long as you respect all the really cool things He does for us," Mom says.

"Does He want us to know that He's there?"

"He always wants us to know that He's watching over us. Now go to bed! What are you going to be? A reporter when you grow up?" Mom starts to tickle me until I erupt in giggles.

"No, but you told me I could ask you the tough questions." Now feeling feisty, lying in bed with my arms crossed, I yell out, "Why can't God *prove* He's here? Grandma Rosie told me that one day you would explain what she meant when she said God was the Sun. What did she mean?"

Mom looks at me and tilts her head to one side. She explains, "Tim, God is the center of our lives. He nourishes us with His loving energy. He trusts us to believe in Him, which is why He gave us the gift of Faith. So you must trust your own faith that He's there. But for those who aren't quite convinced, He proves it every day." She speaks each word slowly: "*God . . . is . . . the . . . Sun.*

"He wakes you up in the morning by illuminating your days. He hugs you with the warmth of His energy. His rays of love allow life on our planet to be possible. Even when the days are cloudy, dark, or rainy, He lets us know that He's still up there. He shines His light brighter behind those clouds, and that's His reminder to us that He's still there.

"And when he wants to thank us for not being upset for allowing Him to water His garden, which is our planet Earth, He thanks us for our understanding by allowing us to see Him sing. Yes, sing! The song is called a rainbow."

I smile as wide as I can as Mom shares with *me* what Grandma Rosie once told *her* when she was a little girl. I feel as if Grandma Rosie is right here in the room with us, helping Mommy remember everything she's supposed to tell me. Now I finally realize what Grandma Rosie meant when she said that God was always there. In each ray of sunlight lives the love I feel for Grandpa, Grandma, Uncle Clyde, and of course, Chester.

I suddenly feel my smile disappear, and I become quiet.

Mom asks, "Honey, what's wrong? Doesn't it make you happy to know that God is always there? Listen to me. Some people search their entire lives, looking for signs that God exists. They seek out other people to follow, change religions thinking that one might be better than the other, and ultimately, they miss the obvious—that He has been with them the whole time. Do you understand?" She pauses. "What's troubling you?"

"Well, does that mean that I should be afraid of the dark? That God isn't watching over me at night?" I ask, fearfully.

"Of course not. At night, when God is shining on the other side of the Earth, showing all His other children the same love and light He shined on us, He leaves us a reminder that He still loves us and watches over us—and it's a very special gift."

"Another *gift?*" I ask.

I look at my mom expectantly as I hear this word, and I also hope that she's about to say something to suppress my fear of the dark. My eyes widen with such anticipation that it looks like I'm listening with my eyes and not my ears.

"Yes, Tim, God gives us many gifts. Everybody is given one when they're born—"

I interrupt and say, "Do you mean poured into the glass?"

"Yes, poured into the glass." She continues, "When we're born, we come in with abilities to teach and share with other people. Some of us can sing, draw, or dance. Some of us might be athletes. Others are given the gift of being physically or mentally challenged. And some—"

"Being challenged is a gift?" I'm so surprised to hear Mommy say this. I guess I'm having a hard time understanding this, after all. How can someone who is born crippled or blind feel like he's got one of God's gifts? This can't be true. There was a boy named Brian who sat in the first row at school last year. He had a disease that made it impossible for him to walk and run like the rest of us. That doesn't seem like any gift *I'd* want.

Now, not certain I can buy any of this, I ask skeptically, "Why would God give us the gift of being challenged?"

With a tone of slight disapproval in her voice, showing her disdain for my criticism of God's gift-giving skills, Mom says, "God gives all of us strengths and weaknesses. Sometimes a person's gift, or challenge, is to help another person show compassion and acceptance. Or maybe, one person's challenge might just help another individual feel gratitude and appreciation for *not* having a challenge.

"Don't you remember Grandma Rosie saying, 'There but for the grace of God go I'? A person who is dealing with a challenge can play the role of teacher for the rest of us. When we stop judging and criticizing others, then the lesson is learned.

We begin to treat everyone as our neighbor, and to love unconditionally."

"Like Chester did? He even wanted to play with Brian at school when I brought him in for Show and Tell last year. He didn't care that Brian couldn't run with him. Is that what you mean?" I ask her.

"Absolutely!" Mom exclaims, with a tone that tells me that she's pleased that I understand. But I can also tell that she's ready for me to stop asking questions. "*Now* are you ready for bed?"

"Wait! What about nighttime then? You didn't tell me about the gift that God gives us at night." I need her to answer the question about the dark—especially before she turns off the light!

"Okay, okay," my tired Mom says, defeated. "I'll explain. You see, when God, the Sun, is shining His warmth on the other parts of our planet, the gift He gives us is the moon. God leaves it there as a placeholder, a reminder, a way to let us know that He's still present, watching over us and protecting us while we sleep—and most important, to remind us that He'll be back the next day."

I smile, finally satisfied with this answer, and I start to blink with heavy eyelids.

Mom tucks me into bed and kisses me goodnight. She walks over to the door, and before she turns off the light, she says one last thing: "And, by the way . . . at night, all those stars you see in the sky, twinkling and shining down upon you—they're all our loved ones in Heaven. Their spirits are shining bright and smiling down on us. That's another gift that God gives us at night. When God isn't illuminating the sky with His light and love, He allows the light and love of our loved ones to do it for Him."

Mom turns off the light and wishes me an early Happy Birthday. I know that she will be in my room in the morning to give me my three very special kisses—one on each cheek, and one on the forehead.

With a smile on my face, I roll over and gaze out the window at an endless stream of stars. As I'm remembering everything that Mom has just told me, I happen to notice three very bright stars twinkling brighter than all the rest. I know without a doubt that Grandpa Jack, Grandma Rosie, and Uncle Clyde are all shining down upon me.

Then I see a shooting star zooming across the sky . . . and at that very moment, I know that it's Chester . . . playing in the fields of Heaven!

❁ ❁ ❁

# Part III

# Chapter Ten

## Going Home

*As I release all the memories of pain and pleasure that have preceded this moment, I leave this place and start to float away. I feel more alive than I have in years. But before I cross over, I have some work to do. I look at my two daughters and my four grandchildren, and I'm filled with such love and gratitude. I know that I must let them know one final thing. . . .*

"Clear!" yells the cardiac technician who is about to jump-start my heart.

Another woman's voice barks, "We're losing him!"

Then I hear the voice of Jamie, the nurse who I think might be an angel in disguise. I hear her yell, "Come on, Tim. Hold on. Don't leave us yet! Don't leave your family!" With a tone bordering on aggravation, Jamie screams out, "Don't leave us, Tim—not today. Not on your birthday!"

This is what it feels like to die. Light. Airy. Easy. I feel myself being lifted out of my body, rising like smoke from a smoldering cigarette. Down below me, I can vaguely hear a fuss being made. They're trying to bring me back, but it's not going to happen.

Wow! This is what I always heard it would be like, and now I'm experiencing it. For all the people who fear this process, I wish that I could personally let them know what a beautiful sensation this is.

I always thought that Melissa and my daughters were crazy for giving credence to soothsayers and psychics and mediums as they tried to connect with their departed loved ones. I thought it was all nonsense. Now, here I am, wanting to scream from the rooftops—or, in my case, room 314—that they were right! I'm still here. I'm not dead. Not my soul, anyway.

I feel like I'm floating. Weightless. As I hover over my old body, I can still see everyone working on me. I'm aware that their efforts are futile, yet they don't seem ready to give up. What they don't understand is that I've made the conscious choice to leave. As I continue to watch these dedicated medical professionals try to save my life, I realize that I'm thinking of the person that they're working on as my *old* body. I think to myself, My *old* body?

To have an "old" anything would imply that there is also a *new* one. So I lift my hands in front of my face, and wonder of wonders, I can still see them. They look the same as they did when I was in the flesh. The frame of my new body looks a lot like the old one, too. It's as if my entire being is lighter—both in weight and color. It almost seems to glow. Now I understand why people look gray when they're at the point of physical death. Their energy, their life glow, which I still possess in this form, has left the old shell of the body.

You'd think that after carting that old body around for as many years as I have, I'd feel some sort of allegiance toward it. Well, I don't. For me, it's like an old pair of shoes that just got too worn, or a car that has a broken transmission. I'm no longer in need of something that can't serve me. I have no emotional attachment to my old physical vehicle.

Maybe I sensed that even before this moment. I mean, I never went to the cemetery to visit any of my relatives who had crossed over. I didn't think that they were actually *there* at the gravesite. Having been raised a Catholic, I believe in Heaven and an afterlife, but I never thought these concepts had anything to do with the physical body. Wow, was I ever right!

I know that as far as everyone else in room 314 is concerned, I'm dying, but frankly, I haven't felt this alive in years. I feel like the doctors gave me a megadose of vitamins, or injected me with some new fountain-of-youth elixir. I feel so energized and vital.

Oh! I just heard a sound that I recognize—probably from watching all those medical dramas on TV. You know, the tone that signals that the person has "flatlined"—that is, they don't have a heartbeat and are . . . dead!

I realize that this is what has just happened to that old shell of a body. It is no longer alive. "I" am now "dead." Of course I know better. How can I be dead when I'm watching all of this happen below me and I'm still thinking and processing ideas?

Death sure isn't the grand finale it's been cracked up to be.

I attempt to speak to the medical team, but they don't hear me. I also try reaching out to touch Jamie, but she has stepped aside, as the team is trying to get my heart started again.

What's interesting about this new state of being is that I can feel the energy and emotions of the people in the room. As I look at Jamie, I can "feel" her despair over my passing. I have the ability to simply "know" information in what seems like milliseconds—almost as if it's being downloaded from an energy computer, and I know it and own it. With Jamie, I'm able to sense that my death is making her reflect on the loss of her own dad. She's reliving the nightmare of losing him, and she's thinking how everything in her life and family changed with his passing.

While I was still in my old body (when I was first admitted with chest pains), Jamie told me that I reminded her of her father, and that we shared the same birthday. (She knew this because it was printed right on my chart and hospital bracelet.) She reminded me that my birthday was coming up in a few weeks, and I asked her how they were going to celebrate *her* dad's birthday.

That was when she told me that she would be celebrating it at the cemetery with her mom and other family members. She smiled thinly while relating the story of how her father was brutally murdered by a deranged drug dealer. She confessed that she had always felt guilty about her dad's death because she'd pulled a double shift that night and didn't have the chance to say good-bye.

She told me back then, "My dad was a cop, and he was due to retire in a year or so. One night he was called in to deal with this strung-out guy who was involved in a domestic dispute. My dad was killed when he tried to intervene in the situation.

"Why was my dad the one who was called in that night? We continually asked that question after the fact, and we were told that because he was not only a cop, but also had his master's in psychology and had a 70 percent success record in these types of situations, they felt he would be the best person for the assignment. Good old Police Officer Ed. Everyone loved him. You should have seen his funeral. The President even called us to offer his condolences. Imagine that."

I had just listened to Jamie without saying anything as she went on with her story. "That man who killed my dad was holding his family at gunpoint and also took the lives of all the other people in his Queens apartment that day. First, he shot his wife and kids, then my father, and eventually himself. It was three years and four months ago, but who's counting." Jamie had smiled sarcastically as she folded my blankets. "I know what I miss the most. I miss him standing behind me and giving me one of his big old hugs. He was notorious for that. He would wrap his arms around me and squeeze me tight, and yell 'big hugs . . . big h—'" Jamie's voice cracked.

I knew that I needed to say something to her then. I took her hand and said, "Jamie, your dad knows how you feel. He's with you, and he's most definitely watching over you." But even as I said those words, I really wasn't certain of the validity of my assurances.

But one thing I did know was that ever since Jamie's father died, whenever a man of his approximate age is facing death, she's forced to deal with her own personal loss again.

As I look down from the vantage point of what feels like the ceiling, I am shocked to be able to see Jamie's father, Police Officer Ed. He's a tall man, proud and smiling, in full uniform, and he's standing right beside his daughter. Not only can I *see* him standing there, but I can also *feel* him! He's sending his energy and love to his daughter in the hopes of being able to get her through this experience in the least painful way possible. He looks over at me and smiles—father to father. I immediately know what he's conveying to me.

He's thanking me for what I had expressed to his baby girl. He's happy that I tried to let her know that he's always beside her, watching over her.

Now, what I wasn't certain of when I said it, I know to be true, because it's happening right in front of me.

Watching Jamie and her dad, I feel like I'm witnessing a miracle. Just as her father puts his energy hand on her shoulders, Jamie instinctively crosses her arms and puts her hands on top of his. It's as if she can feel his warmth and presence. There is a telepathic dialogue happening here, and I'm honored to be witnessing it. Jamie is feeling her dad's energy on her shoulders, just like she remembered. The only thing missing is hearing him say to his daughter, "Big hugs . . . big hugs!"

I don't believe that Jamie realizes on a conscious level that this is taking place and that her dad is here, but on a soul level, she knows it. He looks over at me and smiles. The bond between a father and his daughter, Daddy's little girl, is still as strong as ever, even from the other side.

I now look around the room, and to my left, I can see Mr. Brown (my ex-roommate) sitting behind the pulled curtain. He can hear all the fuss, and he knows that I've probably died. It's amazing that I can now "feel" his emotions and thoughts, too.

They say that when someone loses their eye-sight, their sense of hearing becomes more acute. Well, I've lost all my physical senses, and *all* my spiritual senses are now acute. I can telepathically hear what people are feeling and thinking, and I know that Mr. Brown is concerned—not so much for *me* as for my family.

My family! My thoughts are immediately directed away from Jamie and her dad to my own loved ones. As I think about them, I can *feel* them, and when I look to my right, I'm able to see the beautiful face of my daughter, Rachel. She is stand-ing in the doorway of room 314 with a stricken look on her face as she watches the team of profession-als trying to save her Daddy. Standing there with hot tears streaming down her face, I can feel that she *knows* that I've passed.

I don't want her to be upset, though, because *I'm still here.* I can see her, feel her, hear her, and be with her. I'm not sad, although I can sense her despair. She is wondering why she has to be the only one going through this. (Her twin sister, Vicky, is on the way to the hospital with her husband, Vince, and their three kids.) Rachel's had to go it alone for the last five years since her divorce. What's helped is the support she's received from her daughter, Rose Anne, named for my grandmother. Roro, as we call her, is a strong-willed, inquisitive, high school student who reminds me a lot of myself when I was growing up.

It's no surprise to me that Rachel is the only one here. Since her mom (my wife, Melissa) passed a few years ago, she's taken on the maternal role in the family. Even though my daughters are identical in age, they're *not* in personality. Victoria is not as strong as Rachel. She doesn't deal with stress well, and let's just say that she can't unpack emotional baggage easily. She's been the best wife and mother anyone could ask for, and her husband, Vince, knows it, but he's going to have his hands full dealing with his wife and the kids during this ordeal. However, I know that Rachel will be the one to help them all get through this. She will be my rock—and theirs, too. I only hope that she's able to find her way through this herself.

I know that Vicky wouldn't have been able to handle being the only one here when I left. I also know that I might not have been able to leave my old body as easily if she had been the one at my side. Even though the time was right, I instinctively know that her love for me, her selfish personal need for me to stay (even as sick as my heart was), might have kept me here.

Yes, it all happened perfectly. It was my time to leave, to go home. It was my choice. I know now that it was clearly my soul's choice to pass at the time I did. It's just one of those things that makes complete sense to me now that I've crossed over. I wasn't handed a guidebook here on the other side, nor can I explain it, but there are just realizations that you have in this state of being, things that you just *know*.

I see that the commotion over my old body is winding down. The team has realized that I'm not coming back. Their work is finished.

As the medical team slowly starts to leave the room, Jamie steps forward to make sure that I'm decently dressed before being seen for the last time by my family. She obviously doesn't realize that I'm here, watching her, but I feel her energy and know that this is how she would have dressed her dad if given the chance. After she buttons the top of my pajama shirt and raises the sheet up to my chest, she crosses my arms out in front and lays me down, completely flat. I know that they do this so that the old body doesn't stay in the position that it passed in. Then she takes out my comb and smooths back my hair, kisses my hand, and asks me to say hello to her dad when I meet him.

Mr. Brown suddenly whispers to her, "Pssst. Jamie! Miss Jamie!"

"Yes, Mr. Brown?" Jamie asks vaguely through watery eyes as she opens the curtain separating the two beds.

"He's here, ya know. I saw him!"

"Who did you see?" asks Jamie, almost annoyed.

"The fellow in the next bed, Mr. Callahan. He was floatin' above the bunch of ya, smiling down, looking at all the hubbub and fuss you were all making about him. He was even looking at his own hands. He was watchin' over how ya were treatin' him." Mr. Brown sounds like a child who's talking about an imaginary friend.

"Oh, really?" Jamie asks with complete disbelief. "Well, all right then, Mr. Brown," she says dismissively. "I think I better check to see if it's time for your medication." Then she mutters to herself, "And I think I better check with the doctors because those meds might be making you see things."

As she lifts the water pitcher on Mr. Brown's bedside table so she can fill it, Jamie knows that she can no longer put off the inevitable. She has to tell Rachel, who's back out in the corridor in her favorite "spot," that her dad has just died.

But before she has a chance, Mr. Brown delivers the most profound statement that Jamie has heard in her 18 years of being a nurse—and up to this point, she thought she had seen and heard it all.

Mr. Brown blurts out: "You may not believe me—okay, I *know* you don't believe me, but that's all right. If you don't believe me, the police officer who was standing next to you will tell you. He saw Mr. Callahan, too. *Ask* him."

Mr. Brown's delivery of this message is strong and deliberate. He continues to describe the cop to Jamie, "Go ahead. Ask him. He'll tell you. You know, he's a good-looking guy, that cop, kind of looks like you. Same eyes, and even the same nose." Mr. Brown lets the words tumble out of his mouth, not realizing the effect they're having on Jamie. "I even *heard* him," Mr. Brown continues. "He was

mumbling something about a big bear hug or something like that. . . ."

At that moment, Jamie almost collapses with
joy and amazement, realizing that her dad has come
to give her the strength she needs to deal with the
death of Mr. Callahan, his grieving family, and most
of all, her own feelings of loss. She gazes at Mr.
Brown through her tears, smiles, and then looks up,
uttering a soft, "I love you, Dad . . ."

Wiping her eyes, Jamie pulls the curtain around
the inert body on my bed. She asks the rest of the
team to get their equipment out of the way, because
the family will be coming in shortly.

Jamie steps out into the hall, and I "follow" her
out there. I can see an elderly lady lying on a
stretcher near where Rachel is sitting. She's moan-
ing and crying for help. As I move closer to Rachel
and Jamie's energy, the woman suddenly quiets
down. Oh my God—she can see me! She's smiling
and waving at me. She really sees me! Jamie and
Rachel are watching this inexplicable event take
place, and they look at each other, puzzled.

Rachel says, "I wish I were as out of touch as
she is right now. It would be nice to be oblivious
to everything that's going on."

Jamie sits down next to my beautiful daughter, and they hug for a moment. I can both *hear* and *feel* the words that they express, as well as the sentiments they don't say out loud.

The doors to the unit burst open, and I can see the frantic looks on the faces of my daughter Victoria; her husband, Vince; her twin boys, Mark and Ernie, who are now 11; and her daughter, Anna, who's only 6. She has the cutest cheeks.

Then in walks Roro, and she walks right over to her mom and throws her arms around her.

After each of them goes into 314 to say their good-byes to "me," my entire family stands outside in the hall, wondering what to do next. I watch them embrace, cry, and start the grieving process that so many families endure. It's the same experience that I had to deal with when I lost my parents and my wife. But I know now that as sad a situation as this might be, it's a normal part of the circle of life and love that we all have to go through. There is no escape.

I only wish that I could take away the wrenching pain that my loved ones feel at this moment. I'd like to be able to replace it with the knowledge that I'm alive and okay. I'm still here with them. I can hear them, see them, and feel them!

I remember what my mother once told me when I was a kid—that grief is God's way of helping you explore the love you feel for those who have passed. But now that I have this new perspective on things, my perception of death and grieving is different. Death is not the end. It is merely a transformation. It is a birth to the other side.

I reflect on the fact that the most traumatic experience anyone can go through is his or her own physical birth. Yet we quickly forget the trauma of that experience, because it's what brings us life. I feel that my death is actually my birth, and ironically, they're falling on the same day—my birthday. The day I was born is also the day that I died and was reborn on the other side.

Slowly, my loved ones walk down the hall, leaving room 314 for the last time. As they approach the big double doors of the third-floor cardiac unit, 11-year-old Ernie, the more emotional of Vicky's twin boys, suddenly realizes that he'll never see me, his "Pops," again. That realization hits him hard, and he erupts into hysterical tears. The feelings that he's expressing are those that I know my daughters are experiencing, too, but he's letting them out with the openness and lack of self-consciousness that only a child can feel. Ernie is opening his heart and releasing all his pain for the world (well, the third floor) to hear.

Not quite sure how to deal with this, Vince scoops up his son and holds him in his arms, telling the rest of the family that he and Ernie are going out to the car and that they should all meet out there in a few minutes. Vicky and the girls decide to go, too, but Rachel and Roro stay behind. You can hear Ernie's screams echoing down the corridor as he's carried out.

Jamie tells Rachel that she has to come down to the nurses' station to sign for my belongings. As Roro and Rachel follow Jamie, Roro gently wipes the tears from her mom's eyes and asks her if she's okay. Watching this scene, I'm so moved by their pain. Oh, how I wish I could let them know that I'm all right and still here. I'm still the driver of the car that just broke down! *Hey, down there,* I want to scream. *I'm still alive!*

Roro is telling her mom that she's going to wait for her at the car. She instinctively feels that Rachel isn't ready to leave and needs just one last visit to room 314. I follow Rachel back to my old room, and I see her sit next to my body and weep.

She tells me how much she loves me and how much she'll miss me. She also asks me to say hello to her mom for her. I immediately have the thought that, in death, you become a mailman of sorts, delivering messages to the people who crossed over from the people who are still in human form.

That thought makes me chuckle. So in death, I learn that there's also humor. That's a relief. I've always tried to see the humorous side of life, and to think that there wouldn't be laughter on the other side would be pretty darn depressing. I suppose my sudden spark of humor must have found its way to Rachel, because I can see and feel the energy around her lighten up. She's even lifting her head off my bed and is wiping her tears away. She smiles faintly.

"You always had the ability to make me laugh. I hope you're laughing up there now," a tearful Rachel says.

*She can feel me!* I'm jubilant that my energy is coming through.

"Please help the family get through this. Remember, it was *you,* Dad, who helped us all get through losing Mommy . . . and my divorce. . . . But who's going to help *us* deal with losing you . . . ?" She breaks down and cries again.

I attempt to do for Rachel what Jamie's dad did for *her.* I put my energy hands on my daughter's right shoulder, and I send my girl all the love and strength I can muster.

Rachel stands up and scratches her right shoulder, and I'm thinking that she must be sensing me. But who knows? I'm new at this!

"Happy Birthday, Daddy," Rachel says out loud. "I know that it's normally the person who's having the birthday who receives the gifts, but in this case, I'm going to ask you to give *me* one. Just let me know that you're all right. That's all I need to know. Let me know that you're okay and that you can hear me. Can you do that? If I could just know that, it would help me get through this, and it would help me to help the rest of the family. Just let me know . . . please . . . okay?" She says this last word beseechingly as she walks out of room 314.

I follow my daughter out into the hall and watch her turn left toward the nurses' station to meet with Jamie and sign for my belongings. I need to honor her (and my whole family) by giving her the gift she asked for. I need to let her know that I'm here.

I have to remind her that she was given the same answers that I was about life, love, death, and God as a child. I taught *her* exactly what Grandma Rosie taught my mom . . . and what my mom taught *me* about God being the Sun.

That's when it hits me. I know what I have to do.

# Epilogue

## A Happy Birthday, After All

<u>Rachel:</u>

I'm walking down this hospital corridor for the last time. As I sign for Dad's belongings at the nurses' station, I notice that the time of his death is 8:15 A.M., one hour before the time of his birth. I'm given the plastic bag with his toothbrush, comb, and family pictures in the small frames. I'm trying to be a trooper—brave and strong, like my mom would have been.

As I pass by room 314 again on my way out, I stop and look in once more, noticing the sheet pulled up over his body. It's time for me to go, and I realize that I won't have to deal with the blue-haired Rambos or the money-sucking vending machines anymore. But none of that really means anything. The smallest little things that can really bother you sometimes seem as trivial as can be at a time like this.

Yes, it's time for me to leave this place.

Walking down the corridor, I vaguely note that the old woman on the stretcher who had been kicking up such a fuss earlier is still out there. She really seemed to calm down right about the time that Dad died. They must have given her a shot of something.

As I'm about to walk past her, the old woman suddenly giggles, claps her hands together, and says directly to me, "Honey, your daddy is *here*. He's with you. And he's all right. He's crossing over to be with your momma, honey; he's going to be with your momma and all the rest of your relatives and friends who have crossed. Don't forget that, okay? He wants me to tell you that he loves you more than anything in the world. Go tell your family. He wants you all to know that he'll be watching you from above, sending you his love—always . . ."

I stand next to the woman's stretcher, my mouth hanging open in complete disbelief. Oh my God! This is a miracle. My dad has done it—he has given me the gift I requested by sending a message through this woman on the stretcher!

<u>Tim:</u>

I'm standing behind Rachel, telling the old woman exactly what to say to my beautiful daughter. I just need to let her know that I'm all right, and that she'll be fine, too, and that she doesn't need to wallow in grief or be frightened of dying. But she needs to know one last thing . . . how to help the rest of the family deal with my passing. . . .

I "say" to Rachel through the woman: "Tell the family what Grandma Rosie always said. Tell them that God is the Sun. That will help them all. And tell them . . . that it's beautiful here. . . ."

With that, the old woman starts to cough and gasp for air. Then she starts breathing normally again and closes her eyes to sleep.

<u>Rachel:</u>

I look behind me, hoping that maybe someone else has witnessed this miracle. I want some corroboration that I'm not going crazy. But no one else is around.

Rooted to the floor for a moment, I express my love and gratitude to Dad for delivering this precious gift.

<u>Tim:</u>

I watch my lovely Rachel walk out through the double doors, and I want to follow her. But I find that my ability to move in her direction is hampered, and I'm being pulled back into room 314.

I feel at peace, though. I know that Rachel will share my "last words" with the family, as well as all the important lessons that she learned from me and her mother throughout her life. That knowledge will help all of them deal with my loss. I also know that what we've taught our kids will be passed down to the future generations of my family.

With that, I release my "hold" on life on this plane, and I surrender to the pull upwards.

As I float to the ceiling of room 314, I see the brightest light that I've ever seen. It's drawing me in and calling my name all at once. *This is it!* I think. It's the tunnel that people who have had near-death experiences see. It's as if I'm being pulled by a ray of the sun, a ray of that divine light that Grandma Rosie told me about.

I am now floating through this tunnel of light. The sensation of overwhelming love and peace that I feel can't be put into words.

The "pull" is losing a little strength now, and the light is beginning to take shape and focus. In the distance, I can see a vision of something so familiar. Oh, can it be?! Is it really my dear sweet Melissa coming to greet me?

"Hello, Tim," Melissa telepathically communicates to me. I hear this familiar voice in my head, and it's like music to my ears.

As the light dissipates, I find myself standing at the foot of the driveway of the home I was born and raised in. My darling Melissa is standing there, too, with open arms. She tells me that I was in the hospital for weeks due to severe cardiac heart failure, and that I have been in the process of conducting what is known as a "life review." She says that everyone who leaves his or her body to go "home" must do this.

I feel an overwhelming sense of love emanate from my wife as she goes on to explain, "The life review helps the soul disconnect completely from the earth world. Tim, your review focused on the lessons you learned about love, life, death, and God. Because the deaths of the loved ones in your life had such a great impact on you, it was necessary for you go to back and revisit those times to create a type of closure. In the process of reviewing these lessons, you were able to help your family deal with the pain of your own passing."

As my beloved Melissa takes me by the hand, I realize that we look quite youthful in energy and appearance, almost like we're 30 years old again. Melissa's radiant beauty, coupled with the love she is projecting, is extraordinary. As we stroll up the walk to the door of the home where we shared our lives, Melissa assures me that the family will be fine—and that, together, we will help them make their way through their grief.

We enter our home, and I see that everything is perfect. All the little repairs that I had always wanted to make have been taken care of. But how is that possible?

I notice that there are brilliantly colored, sweet-smelling flowers everywhere. I've never seen vibrant colors like this before. And it's not just my visual senses that are affected. I can actually "feel" the energy and vibration emanating from the flowers.

Yes, I'm really feeling at home now. Melissa steps aside as I walk toward the back of the house, and I see that a party's going on. And, oh, look—there's Uncle Dominick and Aunt Gina. I see Aunt Marsha and Grandpa Jack, too. And, over there, Melissa's mom and dad are sitting together in the corner. Oh, how good it is to see them—I had heard so much about Melissa's parents from my wife, but they had crossed over before we ever had a chance to meet. I now see more of my family members sitting and standing all around the room.

The energy is changing now. It seems that they've all realized that I've arrived. I can sense their thoughts, and they're all welcoming me. Even Mel's father embraces me warmly. I sense his approval of me, as if he's saying, "You were a good husband to my little girl," and I'm touched. I remember how "Jajee Joe" had continued to reach out to his daughter through the "Little Birdie" song that our girls sang to Melissa. That was truly a wonderful gift for a father to give his daughter, and I hope that is how Rachel sees the message I sent to her before I crossed over.

I turn to Melissa to ask her what's happening, but I realize I only need to *think* my thoughts—she senses exactly what I want to know.

"Tim," Melissa tells me, "your loved ones are all here to celebrate your birthday. They've come for you, my dear husband."

I hug the woman I spent my married life with, and then I feel a familiar energy standing behind me. When I turn, Grandma Rosie and Uncle Clyde are standing right in front of me. The sight of them

together makes me so deliriously happy that I don't
know whether to laugh or cry. I know firsthand how
hard Clyde's death was for my grandma, and to see
them together is exhilarating.

Grandma Rosie looks at me and laughs. I know
what she's thinking.

*You're a good student,* she says wordlessly, sending love to me through her eyes and her entire being.

*You were a good teacher,* I respond, returning the
emotions tenfold.

She winks at me.

"Timothy?" I hear my dad's voice. "Welcome
home, son."

My father is holding up a cake with the words
"Happy Birthday, Timothy." And when I see that, we
both start to laugh. We're both remembering how
Cousin Steve wanted his name on all my cakes and
how my dad made sure that *my* day was always just
*my* day.

I look around and realize that Steve isn't here.
Dad explains that when it's Steve's time to come over,
we will all be there for *him*, too.

So that's how it's done over here. Everyone who's
new is greeted by the loved ones who have already
crossed over. It seems like life here on the other side

is just like the girls' birthday party I was remembering earlier. Except that over here, no one has cancer.

I see my mom standing behind my dad now. She looks like the absolute picture of health. She's vibrant, stylish as ever, and envelops me in her loving arms.

My mom beams at me, giving me the special look that she always reserved just for me. She leans in close and kisses me three times—one kiss on each cheek, and one on my forehead. I close my eyes and think how much I've missed this simple gesture. How happy I am to know that's it's really been only a few moments in time since I've been separated from those I love. It's as if that birthday party from so long ago was just yesterday.

Then . . . in the corner of my eye, I see two dogs playing tug-of-war with an old sock! One of them is Jasper, the puppy we gave the girls years ago. And his playmate is my oldest and dearest friend, Chester! I drop to the ground, and with great emotion, I call out, "C'mere, buddy. Want a massage?" I'm so elated to see my Chester that I can barely speak.

My beloved Chester jumps all over me, and I proceed to massage him and hug him and kiss him. He licks my face with gusto, incredibly happy to see *his* best friend, too. . . .

I'm infused with emotion as I view the scene around me. This is the most beautiful place I've ever seen, filled with people and animals whose love makes my heart sing with joy. It's so wonderful to know that our beloved pets are waiting on the other side to meet us, too! This is all so amazing! How could anyone be afraid to die when this is what is waiting for them?

Now I'm feeling a pull deep inside of me. Something's happening. As I quiet my mind, I'm suddenly able to see, hear, and feel my Rachel. She's standing in the hospital parking lot with her family. She's telling them that she's going to share with *them* what Grandma Rosie shared with Pops . . . that God is the Sun.

As she relays this information to the family, a car passes by and beeps its horn three times. Everyone looks up in amazement. They know that when their Pops was a little boy, his mother used to beep her horn for him on his birthday. When he was a father and grandfather, Pops continued the tradition by doing the same thing for *his* family—to symbolize the three kisses he used to get every year on his cheeks and forehead. Much like my wife's father sent posthumous messages to her to bring her comfort, I will find ways to let my family know that I love them and that I'm always spiritually here for them.

<u>Rachel:</u>

What a day! So many thoughts and feelings are going through my head and heart that it's difficult to process them all. But I do know that it's now time for me and my loved ones to get in our cars and go home. Our lives will go on, and we will all be just fine.

With tears in my eyes, I hug my precious family, and I reflect on all the gifts that God has given us. To know that those whom I love are still with me, just on the other side of the veil, gives me tremendous hope and courage. I will pass all of this on to my family.

Right now, as we are all clinging to each other in the asphalt-covered parking lot, one ray of sunlight seems to illuminate the ground beneath our feet.

A thought suddenly comes into my mind, and I "know" that my father is thinking the very same thing at this moment:

*"On both sides of the ray, life and love are eternal. Oh, thank you, God. Thank you. Thank you."*

❁❁❁

❋ ❋ ❋

Look for John Edward's next book
(nonfiction) to be published in April of 2001.

If you have enjoyed *What If God Were the Sun,* John's first inspirational work of fiction, be sure to look for *Final Beginnings* in the near future.

❋ ❋ ❋

# About the Author

John Edward is an internationally acclaimed psychic medium, and the author of the bestselling book, *One Last Time*. He has been a frequent guest on *Larry King Live;* has been the subject of an HBO special; and his TV show, *Crossing Over with John Edward,* airs on the Sci Fi Channel. John publishes his own newsletter and also conducts workshops and seminars for those wishing to develop their own psychic abilities. He lives with his wife on Long Island. His Website is: **www.johnedward.net**.

❀ ❀ ❀

❀ ❀ ❀

We hope you enjoyed this Jodere Group book.
If you would like additional information
about Jodere Group, Inc., please contact:

**Jodere Group, Inc.**
P.O. Box 910147
San Diego, CA 92191-0147
(800) 569-1002

— ❀ —

*Distributed in the United States by:*

Hay House, Inc.
P.O. Box 5100
Carlsbad, CA 92018-5100
(760) 431-7695 or (800) 654-5126
(760) 431-6948 (fax) or (800) 650-5115 (fax)
www.hayhouse.com

❀ ❀ ❀